The Coach U Personal Development Workbook and Guide

The Coach U Personal Development Workbook and Guide

Coach U, Inc.

WILEY

John Wiley & Sons, Inc.

Contents

Acknowledgments

In 1992, the original curriculum for Coach U was authored by Thomas J. Leonard, the person recognized as the founder of the coaching profession. Since Coach U's inception, we have remained committed to regularly updating and improving our materials to remain the leading accredited coach-training organization in the world. There are literally hundreds of seasoned coaches to thank for contributing to the quality of our training materials. One particular individual who deserves recognition is Jodi Jan Shafer, the training director for CoachInc.com. This book would not have been possible without her ongoing focus and dedication.

Each year, we receive many calls and e-mails from our students and graduates, who graciously and generously provide us with input on how to further improve our body of knowledge. Today, our materials truly embody the concept of collective wisdom at its very best. This book is a synergistic product of many minds coming together in collaboration. Although we cannot thank each contributor individually, we sincerely appreciate all of the support that you have given us throughout the years. The comments, suggestions, class facilitation and participation, and coaching experiences that you have shared with us have made a difference. We hope that you are proud of the role that you have played and the contributions that you have made.

Finally, we would like to acknowledge you for considering this book. We know that if you are reading this book, you have an interest in supporting others in their personal and professional development or supporting the growth of organizations. Our vision has always been to have all individuals and organizations on the planet take a coach approach in all forms of communication, whether at home or at work.

We have come a long way since 1996, when we started working together—there were fewer than 500 coaches worldwide. Now, it delights us to know that you, our readers, understand that coaching isn't found just in sports and that coaching is changing the world, one person at a time.

Sandy Vilas
Owner and CEO of CoachInc.com

Jennifer Corbin
Coach U and Corporate Coach U President

Introduction

Imagine if you could wake up on Monday morning, and every morning, excited about the prospects of the day? What if you no longer found yourself just handling life's challenges but actively creating a fulfilling and ideal life? What if you no longer reacted to small annoying things or to large pressing conflicts? What if your relationships, with yourself and others, were as fulfilling as you hoped they could be?

This course literally changed my life. Since I first took the course I ended a marriage to a great guy who was just a friend to me, moved to a geographical area that better suited me, improved my ability to coach my clients as well as my staff, significantly increased my income while eliminating my debt, deepened my relationships with friends and family, remarried into a much more satisfying partnership and more. These things happened because I learned the art of self-care that increased my confidence level and expanded my ability to become more open and able to attract great opportunities.

This program is all about self-care. Some of you might ask, why self-care, what does that have to do with my career or business. What I have learned since I started coaching in 1996 is that if things aren't working at home, they aren't working professionally; if you are experiencing professional challenges, there exist personal challenges as well. I believe that Personal Foundation work is the place to start. Beginning at the foundation will certainly end a lot of start and stops that you might have encountered previously on your path of development. Specifically, these are the concepts that have made a tremendous impact on the quality of my life.

- By handling my *Tolerations* I have more time and space to enjoy since there are fewer distractions in life and in my work.
- I review my personal and professional *Standards* on a regular basis to make sure that they are raised, or lowered, according to what's currently happening in life.
- I speak my *Truth* and set *Boundaries* with others so that we can enjoy the best possible relationship.
- If my *Personal Needs* start affecting my personal or working relationships or cause some sort of other conflict, I am quick to assess the situation and make some modifications.
- I have many fewer complaints since I know that I am responsible for my attitude and have the ability to *Perfect the Present*.

This self-care and personal development program will not support growth and development if you don't take the time to fully work on the concepts presented. This book will support you and provide you with some framework for forward progress. Working with a CoachInc.com trained coach who is well acquainted with these concepts will certainly provide you with additional feedback, support, and accountability. At CoachInc.com we offer a public version of this TeleClass called "Building Your Personal Foundation." Please visit our web site at www.coachinc.com for more information.

All in all, even if you may be able to read through this book in a short period of time, do expect to work on these concepts initially for six to twelve months. And, then just when you think you've got it, you will realize there's more to do. I review these lessons on an annual basis as I continue to raise the bar on the quality of my life and work.

Jennifer Corbin, Professional Certified Coach
Coach U and Corporate Coach U President

Concepts

The Guiding Principles of Human Interaction

What is a "guiding principle?"

A guiding principle is something fundamental about the human condition; a statement that a particular behavior or phenomenon typically occurs, a theory that consistently explains the facts. Guiding principles are like living, breathing things that adapt and grow over time as others test and explore them further. The guiding principles of CoachInc.com also describe an essential aspect of coaching: they speak to what coaches do when they coach and also who they are with their coachees.

How the guiding principles originated

The guiding principles grew out of an ongoing conversation among experienced coaches and the faculty of CoachInc.com. The questions they sought to answer were, "What does it mean to be a coach?" and "What needs does coaching fulfill in the world?" In answering these questions, several fundamental truths about people emerged, beliefs about people that all the coaches shared. These truths became the guiding principles.

The guiding principles are simple, and so basic to human interaction that they typically remain invisible, like the air around us that sustains us. Describing them to people is like describing water to fish. Although they are universally true, each individual has a unique experience of each guiding principle based on his or her cultural and personal history. Therefore, staying true to the collective wisdom, the discussion and exploration of the guiding principles will continue to evolve and grow to explain what it means to be a coach and what needs coaching fulfills in the world.

A guiding principle is something fundamental about the human condition; a statement that a particular behavior or phenomenon always occurs, a theory that consistently explains the facts.

How the guiding principles impact coaching

Each type of coaching has a set of skills associated with it that overlaps with the guiding principles, and all are deeply rooted in love, honoring and valuing one's self and others. Love, honor and valuing one's self and others creates a strong catalyst for change, discovery, and forward movement. These nine types of coaching represent different sides of a prism a coach can look through to see people differently; as such, they also represent nine different frameworks from which a coach can provide value to others.

Guiding Principle	Coaching Base	What It Means
People Have Something in Common	Common-ground-based coaching	Tapping into your own deep love, honor, and value for yourself and others, resulting in a heart-to-heart and respectful connection that invites your coaches to do the same.
People Are Inquisitive	Inquiry-based coaching	Staying in your own wonder and curiosity as long as possible, letting surprising new information appear, rather than jumping quickly to reliable answers and established solutions.
People Contribute	Contribution-based coaching	Acknowledging how those you coach already contribute to others, and assisting them in shaping their contribution to become even better aligned with their purpose and values.
People Grow from Connection	Connection-based coaching	Developing a rich and powerful connection with those you coach that fosters a synergistic flow of creative energy.
People Seek Value	Value-based coaching	Actively listening to those you coach with all of your senses in order to access values that might otherwise remain invisible.
People Act in Their Own Interest	Interest-based coaching	Championing the best interests of those you coach so that they can openly participate in living the life they most want based on their values.
People Live from Their Perception	Perception-based coaching	Creating a larger, more inclusive experience of reality for yourself and those you coach by sharing experiences with each other and living fully in the present.
People Have a Choice	Choice-based coaching	Raising the awareness of choice for those you coach.
People Define Their Own Integrity	Integrity-based coaching	Noticing the level of wholeness and well-being of those you are coaching, and assisting them in gaining an ever-stronger alignment between their calling and their conduct.

	CoachInc.com Guiding Principle	Coach U	Corporate Coach U
1.	People Have Something in Common	We return to the common ground of being by loving, honoring, and valuing others and ourselves.	People are drawn together in companies through a compelling mission and shared vision.
2.	People Are Inquisitive	Wonder, curiosity, and inquiry are the source of all learning.	Organizations that encourage curiosity accelerate learning and creativity.
3.	People Contribute	Contribution based on purpose generates true fulfillment.	When organizations recognize individual contribution, they grow leaders at every level.
4.	People Grow from Connection	Connection is the wellspring of creativity.	Collaboration is the conduit for enhancing people's strengths and generating innovative solutions.
5.	People Seek Value	Listening provides an ever-present access to value.	Listening beyond words is the currency of valuing human capital.
6.	People Act in Their Own Interest	Discernment reveals the opportunities in every situation.	When people link the values of self-interest with self-responsibility, all their interactions improve.
7.	People Live from Their Perception	An inclusive, present-based perception of reality is the platform for effective action.	Recognizing that people perceive reality through their own filters leads to effective communication and creates a platform for positive action.
8.	People Have a Choice	Awareness is the precursor to choice.	Shifting perspectives expands awareness and reveals new choices.
9.	People Define Their Own Integrity	The vigilant development of the fit between calling and conduct creates integrity.	Integrity for individuals comes from continuous alignment between the organization's mission, vision, and values and their own.

COACH U | www.coachinc.com

Intro to Personal Foundation

Overview

○ Benefits Go to Page > 5

By participating in this module, you will learn what a personal foundation is and how it fits into the overall process of personal growth and development. You will learn about Coach U's Personal Foundation program, which is a powerful tool used for personal growth and development.

○ Definitions Go to Page > 6

Personal foundation, personal growth/development, self, integrity, values, needs, wants, goals, priorities, intuition, discern, solutions, environment, shifts, leaps, strengths, symptom, motivation, vision, tolerations, strategy, strategize, and attraction.

○ Concepts Go to Page > 9

What Is Personal Foundation?

An individual's personal foundation is his or her structural basis that supports him or her in living an exceptional life. Just as a house must be built on a strong foundation to avoid collapsing under stress, so must your life. A house's foundation is made up of earth, cement, and steel. Your personal foundation is also made up of three major elements, which we have labeled *What, Who,* and *How.*

Welcome to the Personal Foundation Program

Introduction
Accomplish More, More Easily
Seven Tips to a Stronger Foundation
How to Use the Personal Foundation Program
Lessons
Support Structure
What to Expect
Personal Foundation Program Chart

○ Distinctions Go to Page > 17

No Distinctions are provided in the personal foundation modules.

○ Application

The application section of each personal foundation module will contain the actual lessons that are the personal application and learning for developing a strong foundation. This introductory module contains two lessons—the first and the last.

Let's Get Started!: The Personal Foundation program works better when you take the time to properly prepare for it.

Graduation: Participants will know when they have completed this program. This lesson summarizes and briefly details the learning.

○ Resources

Benefits

By fully participating in the material offered in this section, you will gain an overview of what a personal foundation is and how it relates to the overall process of personal growth and development. You will become familiar with the Personal Foundation program by Coach U, which is a tool that broadens your awareness of how you are currently living your life. This awareness allows you to make choices that are in alignment with your purpose and values, rather than react to circumstances. There are four modules in the Personal Foundation program. This first module is intended as an introduction and reference guide for the other three modules, and should be used in tandem with each of the others.

This introductory module is designed to allow you to:

O **Determine** where a strong personal foundation fits within the context of personal growth and development

O **Discover** how a strong personal foundation allows you to easily accomplish much more

O **Begin** to understand the path most conducive to developing a strong personal foundation

O **Have** a reference piece for your work through the Personal Foundation program

Definitions

The following are common words used to gain a better understanding of the coaching process, particularly in regard to strengthening personal foundation. Most of these definitions are found in other Coach U modules but are considered a valuable reference for personal foundation and, as such, are presented in this introductory module.

Personal Foundation: A structural basis to support an individual in living an exceptional life. As defined by Coach U, one's personal foundation is composed of three elements: the *What*, the *Who*, and the *How* of a person (refer to the Concepts section of this module).

Personal Growth/Development: Personal growth and development is the overall process of evolving your life to fully express your purpose and values.

Self: Our "self" is who we are versus the terms we use to label ourselves. It is our distinct personality that creates our individuality. We draw on this self as we are called upon to respond to the world.

Integrity: Integrity is a state of personal wholeness, well-being, and fulfillment—not something to achieve, but rather a statement of our being. It is a reflection of who you are in any moment and is the dynamic relationship you maintain between purpose and path. It is the vigilant development, or continual adjustment, of the fit between our calling and conduct that allows us to sustain a high level of integrity.

Values: Values are ideals that are personally important and meaningful for you and draw you forward. Values are inherent in each person's makeup; we all have them. They are specific and individual, but people can share common values. For example, people often value honesty, openness, and respect in a conversation.

Needs: Needs are the emotional aspects that drive individuals. The driving force behind needs is based in human yearning for wholeness. Often, needs direct major life decisions until they are met. Needs can also sit on top of, or get in the way of, a person's clearly identifying their values and living life based on those values. The kinds of needs we are discussing here go beyond the basic needs for food, air, water, and shelter to the things that a person feels they must have. For example, clients may need to be accepted, to accomplish, to be acknowledged, to be loved, to be right, or to be cared for.

Wants: To want something is to wish for it or desire it. Wants are flexible and/or optional; if you get it, great; if not, you are still okay. When your needs are met and your life is oriented to your values, your wants tend to proportionately decrease. For example, a person may want to succeed in business, have a great body, or have a big house.

Goals: A goal is the objective of a strategy. A goal can be very simple or extremely complex. It is the result or achievement, toward which effort is directed: the aim or end of something. A goal implies that work (or effort) is involved to achieve it.

Priorities: A priority is something that takes precedence over something else: something given special attention. In general, priorities are a set of ideals (physical, spiritual, or emotional), that when grouped together compose the items most important to an individual. They are considered to be at the top of any list of things to achieve in any area of life.

Intuition: This is the perception of truth, facts, information, or other input not based on any reasoning process. It is the ability to have insight into something based on our own inner knowledge and truth, and not on external stimulus.

Discern: This means to be able to perceive and distinguish between things, usually through intuition or other internal knowledge. It means to recognize contrasts such as good and bad, right and wrong, timely and untimely, truth and untruth, real and false. Discernment is the natural ability to discern.

Solutions: The answers and/or solution to a particular problem, situation, challenge, or dilemma. For example, a common solution to miscommunication is to clarify what you hear the other person saying.

Environment: An environment is the aggregate or combination of surrounding things, conditions, and influences, including social, cultural, relational, personal, and professional forces, that shape the life of a person.

Shifts: Literally, a shift is a transfer from one place or position to another and includes a change, exchange, or substitution of something. It means to put something aside, such as a concept or understanding, and replace it with another. A shift can be systematic, following an established path of growth, or it can happen suddenly. Shifts are observable in resulting behaviors.

Leaps: To leap is to literally "spring" from one point or position to another. It involves jumping or springing over something to get to another place. In personal development, a leap is sudden and quick, not following a prescribed pattern of growth, and is usually accompanied with dramatic evidence of the leap. Leaps can be made over short or extensive distances. Leaping is the most obvious of all forms of client development observed by a coach.

Strengths: Literally, strength is the quality or state of being strong, an intellectual or moral force, a source of power, an attribute, or something with great value. Strengths are a collection of attributes, those things that a person excels at doing or has natural ability for. Strengths can be physical, emotional, or spiritual; they are values, skills, talents, attitudes, relationships, resources, and other sources of power, sustenance, encouragement, and satisfaction.

Symptom: The visible expression of a condition or situation; something that indicates the presence of something else. For example, if your client is speaking very quickly, he or she may be upset or not sure of what to say.

Motivation: An incentive or inducement to action. For example, a client may work hard at improving her communication skills because she wants to be promoted at work.

Vision: A vision is simply something seen. A personal vision is something seen for the future. It involves anticipation, foresight, perception conception, and desire. It is a scene of being for the future. A personal vision is based on wants, needs, values, and goals. A vision may be singular in nature or involve many facets.

Tolerations: To tolerate means to allow the existence of something, to permit or endure something, to put up with something. This implies that the something (or someone) is less than desirable, less than the ideal, and tends to drain a person's energy. A toleration is a situation, a condition, an influence of any kind that is allowed to exist, is put up with, that is less than ideal. A toleration is often a hindering influence.

Strategy: A strategy is simply a plan or a method for achieving a specific goal. A strategy can be anything from a way to accomplish a simple task to a way to live life more fully. Strategies generally have several ways they identify and track the goal-seeking process. A good strategy is one that makes use of all available resources.

Strategize: To develop a strategy, plan, or method for achieving goals.

Attraction: To be drawn to something. In coaching, attraction is the power and ability to draw people or circumstances to oneself. Being open to acting on one's intuition allows a person to attract the right clients for the right fit.

❝ Reputation is what you are perceived to be.
Character is what you are. **❞** | **John Wooden**

Concepts

What Is Personal Foundation?

An individual's personal foundation is his or her structural basis that supports them in living an exceptional life. Just as a house must be built on a strong foundation to avoid collapsing under stress, so must your life. A house's foundation is made up of earth, cement, and steel. Your personal foundation is also made up of three major elements.

Humans are complex creatures. Volumes have been written about the various components, physical and otherwise, that comprise an individual. Essentially, however, all that we are can be summed up in three parts we often call body, mind, and spirit. To simplify the understanding of these parts, and ultimately the refining and growth of the whole, this personal foundation program will label them the *What, Who,* and *How* of every person.

The *What*

We have called this part *What,* as it aptly labels the presenting "package" of a person. It is *What* the world sees when it looks at us. This element is also composed of several sub-elements, or parts, as well. We can include such things as behavior, the public self, what we show others. The *What* can be related to the "body" part of the body, mind, and spirit model.

The *Who*

The *Who* part of you is easily understood as the real you, the core of who you are in reality, not in presentation of the *What*. The *Who* often drives the *What*, but is not always consistent with it. The *Who* can also be identified with the "spirit" part of the body, mind and spirit analogy.

The *How*

The third component of personal foundation is the set of processes, methods, and values that drive our behavior—*How* we do the things we do, and *How* we are *Who* we are. The fuel for the *How* of us is the *Who*, which essentially yields the *What*. If you put this into an equation it would look like this: *Who* + *How* = *What*. The *What* equates to the "mind" part of body, mind, and spirit.

Every person on this planet shares a common composition and the similar desires for development. Just understanding this, that common ground of being, allows for great advancements in coaching, or any other kind of relationship.

Guiding Principle 1	**People Have Something in Common.** We return to the common ground of being by loving, honoring, and valuing self and others.

It is our opinion that people desire to participate in this or other personal foundation programs because they want more value in life, because they want to contribute something more, and because they understand that people grow from connection.

All nine of the CoachInc.com Guiding Principles have direct and useful application to this personal foundations program, and it is helpful to review them before beginning. Review the CoachInc.com Guiding Principles Reference Chart.

Guiding Principle 2	**People Are Inquisitive.** Wonder, curiosity, and inquiry are the source of all learning.

Ultimately, people have a choice. They choose to stay the way they are, or they choose to improve and grow through personal effort, discovery, and development. Awareness is the beginning of choice. If you are participating in this program, you have become aware that you can become more than you are right now. You can, and this program will be the beginning of a lifelong pursuit of excellence in life.

Guiding Principle 8	**People Have a Choice.** Awareness is the precursor to choice.

This program is a robust tool that creates the awareness you need to make powerful choices for your life. It is important to acknowledge that there is absolutely nothing wrong with you the way you are right now. Strengthening your personal foundation is not a requirement. Rather, it is an opportunity to deepen your level of intimacy with yourself. Personal foundation work creates a multifaceted reflection of the self. We tend to see and understand ourselves in a very narrow definition. From this increased awareness, you are free to make the choices that lead to the personal fulfillment that comes from aligning your actions with your purpose and values.

The Path of Development
The process of building a strong personal foundation teaches you how to identify the source of many common problems that are usually thought of as an expected part of life. By moving forward with a stronger foundation, many of these problems can be prevented or entirely eliminated. Since you no longer must focus on the fundamentals, you are free to focus on fully using your unique gifts, talents, and strengths.

At any given time, you can assess your progress by referring to the path of development that begins with restoring yourself, after healing from past experiences, and then travels through strengthening your personal foundation and ultimately leads to leaving a legacy. It is important to acknowledge that every individual is on a unique timetable for personal growth and development. When you are ready, you will enhance your development by moving through the various lessons. Initially, it's most important to gain awareness of exactly where you are on the path.

A strong personal foundation is the first major milestone on the path of development. A strong personal foundation is not created overnight.

This is a Process

The Personal Foundation program is a process that requires time and energy. The ideal starting point is with lessons related to the *What* because they tend to be objective and linear in nature and usually clear the path for other work that is ahead. This is the equivalent of a painter preparing a canvas for a painting. It may not be glamorous, but it creates the best condition for a beautiful creation. Many of the things we choose to address are things that we have been living with for a very long time. This stage of personal foundation requires acceptance, courage and open-mindedness. Unfortunately, it is not surprising that many people are tempted to skip over this section, or even stop at this point. Don't stop. The destination is well worth the difficulty of the journey.

The following information relates to the reasoning, logistics, structure, and content of the program.

Welcome to the Personal Foundation Program

Before we begin, please note that throughout this program you will see references to coaches and working with a coach. This program was developed by and for coaches to use with their clients. If you do not have a coach and would like to work with one, ask the person who gave you this program for a referral to a coach, call the free coach referral service at 1-800-48COACH, or visit our online coach referral service at www.findacoach.com.

Introduction

Virtually every person who engages a coach wants more, sometimes much more, and knows that they must make certain changes in their personal and professional lives in order to get more of what they really want. These changes take time, coaching and effort. You focus on the process of strengthening the client's personal foundation as a way to accelerate and attract more easily the client's goals. The personal foundation process involves deliberately investing in self, usually far more than the client has done before or thinks he/she needs, deserves or should. You ask the client to become very, very selfish (not egotistical, ego-centered, consuming or needy; rather, a self-advocate and practice self-care).

The process is done by engaging in conversations and putting into place the following components of an individual's personal foundation:

- Get clear of the past using Coach U's Clean Sweep program
- Eliminate tolerations
- Get core needs met, once-and-for-all
- Identify and reorient around the client's true values
- Establish extensive boundaries, but not walls
- Substantially raise the client's personal standards
- Learn how to instruct others and educate one's environment
- Set up what we call S.A.S.S. (Selfish Automatic Sprinkler Systems)
- Resolve any blocks or conflicts with the client's immediate and extended family
- Develop a supportive, lifetime community

Not a small order!

You learn what these elements of the personal foundation are and how to weave these in with the goals, concerns and reasons that brought the client to you in the first place. *(Remember, the client rarely comes to a coach requesting a strong personal foundation, nor will the client put their goals on hold in order to exclusively work on this. So, you must master the process of including these personal foundation conversations and activities along with the client's primary goals.)*

Accomplish More, More Easily

You will accomplish more, more easily if you take the time to first strengthen your personal foundation.

Who doesn't want to accomplish more in life? Don't most of us want more time? More money? More love? More satisfaction? Yet, our tendency is to search for it rather than simply having it all come to us. A strong personal foundation includes 10 distinct stepping stones which, when linked together, provide a solid, yet personalized base on which to build your life, and a way to naturally attract the things you want. And, in a world, which sometimes appears to be built on quicksand, we all need a solid, dependable personal foundation.

These 10 stepping stones are:
1. A past that is fully complete.
2. A life that is based fully on integrity.
3. Needs that have been identified and fully met.
4. Boundaries that are ample and automatic.
5. Standards that bring out your best.
6. An absence of tolerations.
7. A choice to come from a positive place.
8. A family that nurtures you.
9. A community that develops you.
10. A life fully oriented around your true values.

Anyone who is living a meaningful life must have a strong personal foundation so they can afford to look up at the stars instead of down at their feet. Having a strong personal foundation allows a person to fully use their skills and resources. A master coach is uniquely trained to help clients strengthen their own foundation, and is a model of how well the process works.

A skyscraper doesn't start at street level. In fact, the taller the building, the deeper the foundation. This holds true for people, too.

Seven Tips to a Stronger Foundation

The following chart includes some very valuable tips and hints for approaching and working through the Personal Foundations program. You will most likely also develop your own tips for a more personal experience.

Seven Tips to a Stronger Foundation		
1.	Understand that a personal foundation is an investment in your personal infrastructure.	To grow tall, we must be anchored on bedrock, not quicksand. We have to go deeper "inside." It generally requires one to three years and is a once-in-a lifetime investment (like a degree) that pays off forever.
2.	There will be major changes in your life during this process.	You will start telling and living the truth more and putting yourself first; this takes lots of practice. You will re-prioritize how you spend your time and energy: warn people around you. Realize that you are remodeling, using new materials and the architect's plan may be initially fuzzy. You will hit soft and hard spots (resistance) as you strengthen the structure; do not stop.
3.	It's okay to complain, as long as you're working.	Vent the frustrations or emotional reactions you have along the way; your coach understands. Keep learning those annoying lessons fully, especially if they keep coming at you! Understand that you are doing your very best, even if you have to catch your breath along the way.
4.	Go all the way with your rebuilding, not "just far enough."	If you are making changes, don't do them just "so far," but be wise about it and do them incrementally as you feel comfortable. Don't rush it, but keep going steadily, and go far. Do the maximum in work: make sure whatever you are building will not crumble. Do it totally "your way" even if that means making mistakes. Use your own plan, not someone else's.
5.	Work the personal foundation 10-step program.	You do not need to reinvent the wheel; the program works. Adapt it to your needs, but don't change it. Get at least one to three points each week in the 100-point program. Set aside time each week. Use the companion programs for help: Clean Sweep, NeedLess, Tru Values.
6.	Stop tolerating anything.	You will know you are strengthening your personal foundation when you stop putting up with things you once tolerated. Don't let people drain, disturb or diminish you. Don't put up with your own silly behavior. You will find yourself *growing*. Make changes.
7.	Graduate and move on to the next level of programs.	When you reach 80 on personal foundation, start working on Coach U's Buff It Up!, Personal Path, and Advanced Personal Development. Make sure your physical environment now reflects your graduation: people, home, money, and life. Celebrate your accomplishment. Congratulations!

How to Use the Personal Foundation Program

You are starting a deliberate process to strengthen every part of your personal and professional life. You should be excited and ready to do this. If not, find out why not and fix that. Hundreds of people just like you have used this program and have helped us to make it user-friendly, effective and fun. You will be focusing on you for the next six or twelve months, building yourself and your life from the inside out so that it becomes sustainable, easier and more rewarding. The Personal Foundation program is a comprehensive, coordinated approach to significantly enhance the quality of your life. You will not be the same after completing this program.

Lessons

This program is organized into individual lessons. Each lesson:

- Focuses you on an area of your personal foundation
- Educates you on this area
- Helps you to identify the actions, changes and shifts to make
- Creates a game out of completing each lesson (the personal foundation chart)
- Points you to the next lesson

The lessons will be found in the "Application" section of each of the four modules.

Each lesson has three parts: A, B, and C. As you complete each part, look for the "Credit" icon that reminds you to color in that applicable area of your personal foundation chart. Post this chart somewhere where you will see it daily and feel inclined to work on it.

You do not need to do each lesson completely before working on another, nor must you work the lessons in order. You should start working wherever it feels best to you, although you will need to complete all lessons in order to graduate from the program and enjoy the benefits.

Lessons Included
There are a total of four modules that make up the Personal Foundations program. This is the introductory module. In addition to the basics and concepts behind the Personal Foundation program, it also contains two of the lessons—the first and the last. The other three modules contain lessons grouped into the three areas of personal foundation, *What*, *Who*, and *How*.

Introduction to Personal Foundation

Let's Get Started! (My Theme)
Graduation

Personal Foundation Level 1
(The *What*)

Zap the Tolerations
Get Yourself Clear of the Past
Create and Use 10 Daily Habits
Simplify Your Life Dramatically

Personal Foundation Level 2
(The *Who*)

Restore Your Integrity
Get Your Needs Met
Extend Your Boundaries
Raise Your Standards
Strengthen Your Family

Personal Foundation Level 2 continued...

Deepen Your Community
Be Well Protected
Become a Problem-Free Zone

Personal Foundation Level 3
(The *How*)

Reorient Around Your Values
Invest in Your Life
Choose Your Work to Be You
Choose a Healthy Attitude
Create a Reserve
Start Attracting
Perfect the Present

Support Structure

This program is not easy; in fact, it is quite challenging. It is so challenging that you would be wise to arrange for a support structure to help you complete the program more quickly and to have a much more enjoyable time as you work the program.

Effective support structures include:

- *Working with a PF-trained Coach.* Your Coach U trained professional coach has been there and can help you through this.
- *Community.* Invite others to do this program with you; there is encouragement and mutual support in a group.
- *Teaching.* Teach this program to others; this deepens your personal understanding, and generates natural support and additional learning.

What to Expect

During the coming months, here are some of the things that you can expect to happen. All of these things might not happen to you, but many will. They are that predictable.

- Your priorities will change. What you thought was important will be less or even more so.
- Your friends/community will upgrade. You may even lose several friends or colleagues.
- You will take better care of yourself, even if you are taking good care of yourself now.
- You will have more energy, though at first you might be dragging.
- You will be discouraged. Remember, you are making fundamental changes.
- You will expect more of others, and of yourself. You may even get demanding.
- Your life will get simpler, easier, and less stressful.

Well, there you have it—some of the things to expect during and after this program. The best way to enjoy these changes is to understand that you are putting yourself first in this program and that this will both ripple and ricochet. Have patience with others and have compassion for yourself. Keep going, even when you are not sure why or how. You will be sure, eventually.

Personal Foundation Program Chart				
A	B	C	Personal Foundation Lesson	
			Let's Get Started! (My Theme)	Intro
			Zap the Tolerations	Level One
			Get Yourself Clear of the Past	
			Create and Use 10 Daily Habits	
			Simplify Your Life Dramatically	
			Restore Your Integrity	Level Two
			Get Your Needs Met	
			Extend Your Boundaries	
			Raise Your Standards	
			Strengthen Your Family	
			Deepen Your Community	
			Be Well Protected	
			Become a Problem-Free Zone	
			Reorient Around Your Values	Level Three
			Invest in Your Life	
			Choose Your Work to Be You	
			Choose a Healthy Attitude	
			Create a Reserve	
			Start Attracting	
			Perfect the Present	
			Graduation	Intro

A B C

Credit ●○○

Remember to color in or check the boxes marked A, B, and C of each lesson, whenever you see the "Credit" icon throughout this book, as you work your way through this program.

Distinctions

Because of the somewhat different nature of the contents of the personal foundation modules, no "Distinctions" are provided here. The lessons contained in the "Application" section of each of the four personal foundations modules are relatively self-contained and self-explanatory.

Application

Let's Get Started! (My Theme)

Key Points

1. This process takes about a year.
2. Start wherever you would like.
3. Don't push it; just progress naturally.
4. Prepare to see/get used to fundamental changes.
5. Let others know that you are doing this.
6. Work with a Coach U trained coach who has experience with Personal Foundation for guidance.
7. Use the Personal Foundation program workbook.

Introduction

The Personal Foundation program works better when you take the time to properly prepare for it. Follow these three steps and work your way through this introductory lesson. Concept lessons begin in Level One.

Area A: Personal Readiness

Completion of the Personal Foundation program is not easy. It is not something that you can do quickly, hastily, or without a great deal of forethought and planning. It is challenging, and will require a full commitment from you for the work involved, and the time it will take to do it. Before beginning this program, it is very helpful to spend a few moments contemplating your readiness for it. Give thought to the following questions and briefly respond in the spaces provided.

Readiness Questions

1. Do you have the physical time it will take to complete this program? Are you prepared to give the program a priority in your schedule? Why is *now* the right time?

_____

_____

_____

_____

2. What might you have to remove from your schedule or priorities in order to do this program? Are you perfectly willing to do so? What sacrifices will you have to make in order to devote your time to this? Are you ready for these?

3. Are you emotionally ready to honestly deal with exploring the *What, Who,* and *How* of yourself? Is there anything else in your life right now that will demand more of you emotionally, and may prevent you from being fully committed to this endeavor?

4. Have you given thought to your own personal approach to this program? In other words, have you looked realistically at how you will accomplish it (practicalities such as time of day, how much per day, order, expectations for completion, etc.)?

5. Are you physically healthy right now? If not, how might that interfere with your ability to complete the program?

6. What positive, healthy energy and strength sources exist in your life currently that will help you see this program through to completion, especially in those moments when you might struggle with certain lessons? Be specific and identify them for future reference.

_____

_____

_____

_____

_____

7. What are your personal expectations, desired benefits and outcomes that you hope to achieve by completing this intensive program? List as many as you can think of. It is helpful to compare this list to the actual benefits list you will compile upon completion of the program.

_____

_____

_____

_____

_____

Now, go back and review this list. Is there anything in your responses that may prevent you from successfully and wholeheartedly committing to and completing the Personal Foundation program? If so, perhaps it is time to clean up the distractions or hindrances you have delineated. If not, let's get started!

A B C

Credit ●○○ When you have completed this exercise, give yourself credit by filling in **Area A** of this lesson on the personal foundation chart. _(These "Credits" will be common to all lessons. Each Lesson will have Area A, Area B, and Area C. You will be asked to darken in the boxes of the appropriate A, B, or C on the personal foundation chart each time you complete an area.)_

Area B: Theme

Making a game out of the Personal Foundation program makes it more fun and more personal. And part of making it a game is to create a theme that makes the program come alive and be yours. Create a theme that fits for you. Once you know what it is, write it on the personal foundation chart. You can always update it later.

Personal Foundation Idea Bank
- My way, all the way.
- It's *my* life and I'm going to prove it!
- Integrity first, needs second, wants third.
- The next six months are for me!
- Day by day, it's something new!
- I am going to soar in 2006!

You get the picture. Create a theme that inspires, motivates, and orients you for this program.

A B C

Credit ○●○

When you have completed this exercise, give yourself credit by filling in **Area B** of this lesson on the personal foundation chart.

Area C: Support

It matters who and what you will use to support yourself throughout this program. It is easier to get through this program and enjoy yourself, with several support structures. Pick from the list below, or create your own support structure. Be sure to inform the people who will be your support team of what you will be doing and how you would like them to support you.

Personal Support
- Coach
- Spouse
- Family
- Best friend
- Girl/Boyfriend
- Boss
- Staff
- Special focus/support group
- Church group
- Department
- Selected customer

External Support
- Personal foundation chart on the wall
- Weekly meetings
- Setting up a reward for each lesson
- Creating a consequence (without an element of "punishment")
- Setting a goal that requires a strong foundation

Credit A B **C** ◯ ◯ ●

When you have completed this, give yourself credit by filling in **Area C** of this lesson on the personal foundation chart.

Congratulations! Now you have started.

Graduation!

Save this section for when you have completed all the lessons in all four personal foundation modules. Return to this area to finalize your graduation.

Key Points

1. Feel ready to complete this program.
2. Review each lesson and complete the details.
3. List the changes made and how you benefitted.
4. Pass around this program to at least three people (optional).
5. Decide if you wish to start on an advanced program (Buff, Attraction, etc.).
6. Determine how you will strengthen others as a result of completing this program.

Introduction

You will know when you have completed this program. Please take the time to finalize your personal foundation journey by working through the three areas of this lesson.

Area A: Review Each Lesson

Please skim through your notes for each lesson in this workbook and write down your three most significant and beneficial notes for each.

Area A: Review Lessons		
Lesson		**Most Significant Notes**
Introduction to Personal Foundation		
Let's Get Started!	1	
	2	
	3	
Personal Foundation Level 1		
Zap the Tolerations	1	
	2	
	3	
Get Yourself Clear of the Past	1	
	2	
	3	
Create and Use 10 Daily Habits	1	
	2	
	3	
Simplify Your Life Dramatically	1	
	2	
	3	

Personal Foundation Level 2		
Restore Your Integrity	1	
	2	
	3	
Get Your Needs Met	1	
	2	
	3	
Extend Your Boundaries	1	
	2	
	3	
Raise Your Standards	1	
	2	
	3	
Strengthen Your Family	1	
	2	
	3	
Deepen Your Community	1	
	2	
	3	
Be Well Protected	1	
	2	
	3	
Become a Problem-Free Zone	1	
	2	
	3	
Personal Foundation Level 3		
Reorient Around Your Values	1	
	2	
	3	
Invest in Your Life	1	
	2	
	3	
Choose Your Work to Be You	1	
	2	
	3	
Choose a Healthy Attitude	1	
	2	
	3	
Create a Reserve	1	
	2	
	3	

Start Attracting	1	
	2	
	3	
Perfect the Present	1	
	2	
	3	
Introduction to Personal Foundation		
Graduation!	1	
	2	
	3	

A B C

Credit ⦿◯◯

When you have completed this exercise, give yourself credit by filling in **Area A** of this lesson on the personal foundation chart.

Area B: Benefits

Please list 10 specific benefits you have received from completing this program.

1. _____

2. _____

3. _____

4. _____

5. _____

6. _____

7. _____

8. _____

9. _____

10. _____

A B C

Credit ⊙●⊙ When you have completed this exercise, give yourself credit by filling in **Area B** of this lesson on the personal foundation chart.

Area C: Service

Part of maintaining a strong personal foundation is strengthening the people around you. Please list how you have—or how you will—strengthen others through your completion of this program.

_____

_____

_____

_____

_____

_____

_____

_____

A B C

Credit ⊙⊙● When you have completed this, give yourself credit by filling in **Area C** of this lesson on the personal foundation chart.

Congratulations!

Guiding Principle 3 | **Contribution based on purpose generates true fulfillment.**

Resources

Attention Readers:

Thank you for participating in the collective wisdom of Coach U. Together, we all continue to learn. Additional resources and forms can be found in the *Coach U's Essential Coaching Tools: Your Complete Practice Resource* book by Coach U, Inc.

Attention CoachInc.com Students and Graduates:

CoachinInc.com students and graduates may find additional and/or more recent resources associated with this module in the resource area of the student-only website. If you are a student or graduate of one of CoachInc.com's ICF-accredited coach training programs, you can access these by searching under the name of the course. When the course description page appears you may find a link to the list of additional resources. Each item is a live link to its actual location on the website. Click on the item to access the information.

Do remember to take the associated online self-test for this module once you have completed the course in-person or by TeleClass. The tests are required for coach certification with the International Coach Federation. Throughout the course or anytime you find valuable resources for a particular course, please feel free to add to the value of our curriculum by forwarding the resource to revampteam@coachu.com.

www.coachinc.com

Personal Foundation
Level 1

Overview

Benefits
Go to Page > 33

By fully participating in the material offered in this Personal Foundation Level 1 module, you will be significantly strengthening and improving your personal foundation through work on the *What;* the public behavioral representation of self.

Definitions
Go to Page > 34

Please refer to the Definitions section of the Introduction to Coach U's Personal Foundation module.

Concepts
Go to Page > 35

What is Personal Foundation?: The *What* Component
Your personal foundation is your structural basis that supports you in living an exceptional life. The *What* of Personal Foundation aptly labels the presenting "package" of a person. It is *What* the world sees when it looks at you.

Distinctions
Go to Page > 37

No Distinctions are provided with this module.

Application
Go to Page > 38

The Application section of each personal foundation module will contain the actual lessons that are the personal application and learning for developing a strong foundation. This module contains the four lessons relating to the *What* component of personal foundation.

> **Zap the Tolerations**: Tolerations are those things that you put up with every day that distract you from what is most important.

> **Get Yourself Clear of the Past:** Getting yourself clear of the past means that you are addressing previously unresolved matters.

Create and Use 10 Daily Habits: The 10 Daily Habits routine will keep you focused, clear, motivated and moving forward.

Simplify Your Life Dramatically: We are all too busy. It's contagious. When your schedule is too full, you miss out on life. Growth occurs faster when there is space.

○ Clean Sweep Program

Go to Page > 57

○ Resources

Go to Page > 64

Benefits

By fully participating in the material offered in this Personal Foundation Level 1 module, you will be significantly strengthening and improving your Personal Foundation through work on the *What* component. You will learn how to eliminate roadblocks to personal growth, improve your attitude and create new and healthy habits which support you in making choices that are more aligned to who you really are.

This module is designed to allow you to:

O **Work** through four lessons that will dramatically affect the *What* of your Personal Foundation—what the world sees when it looks at you

O **Discover** how you can significantly identify and reduce stress and clear much of the mental clutter in your life

O **Remove** tolerations that limit your growth

O **Do** the groundwork necessary to build awareness that is supportive and informative of all the remaining lessons found in the personal foundation program

Definitions

Please refer to the Definitions section of the Introduction to Personal Foundation module.

Concepts

What Is Personal Foundation?: The *What* Component

Most of the following information, relevant to the What *of the 3-part personal foundation, is provided from the Introduction to Coach U's Personal Foundation module. Please refer to this introductory module for further information about personal foundation.*

Your personal foundation is the structural basis that supports you in living an exceptional life. Just as a house must be built on a strong foundation to avoid collapsing under stress, so must your life. A house's foundation is made up of earth, cement and steel. Your personal foundation is also made up of three major elements.

Humans are complex creatures. Volumes have been written about the various components, physical and otherwise, that comprise an individual. Essentially, however, all that we are can be summed up in three parts we often call body, mind, and spirit. To simplify the understanding of these parts, and ultimately the refining and growth of the whole, this personal foundation program will label them the *What, Who,* and *How* of every person.

This module contains lessons relating to the What *of personal foundation.*

The *What*

The *What* aptly labels the presenting "package" of a person. It is *What* the world sees when it looks at us and is most obvious to the individual. This element is also composed of several sub-elements, or parts, as well, including such things as behavior, the public self, what you show others. The *What* is not limited to physical or physically apparent signs as seen by others, but also includes layers just beyond the obvious such as labels, complaints, problems, symptoms, situations and styles. The *What* of a person is usually what is addressed first when beginning a program like this, or when first engaging a coach. It is what is seen first, what is immediately known or discovered about a person, and what a client often identifies as needing the most attention.

One of the tools available to you, and foundational to the Coach U training, is the Five-S Model which the coach will use with a client during the evaluation and development of that individual. The symptoms and situations sides of this model directly apply to this personal foundation section— the *What* of the person. During your work through this personal foundation program, you will be guided to a view of the symptoms and situations in your life that can be developed, refined, solved or even eliminated. After completing the work in this program, the *What* of you will be much different than when you began. What you present to the world will be free of clutter, contrasting behavior, styles and image. Your symptoms of problems, and negative situations will be much reduced to a slimmer, more efficient and streamlined *What* of you.

The Application section of this module contains the lessons pertaining to the *What* of the personal foundation and includes:

- Zap the Tolerations
- Get Yourself Clear of the Past
- Create and Use 10 Daily Habits
- Simplify Your Life Dramatically

" Character cannot be developed in ease and quiet. Only through experience of trial and suffering can the soul be strengthened, vision cleared, ambition inspired, and success achieved. " | **Helen Keller**

Distinctions

Because of the somewhat different nature of the contents of the personal foundation modules, no "Distinctions" are provided here. The lessons contained in the "Application" section of each of the four personal foundation modules are relatively self-contained and self-explanatory.

Application

This section is composed of four different lessons:

- Zap the Tolerations
- Get Yourself Clear of the Past
- Create and Use 10 Daily Habits
- Simplify Your Life Dramatically

Work your way through all four lessons and be sure to color in the appropriate "CREDIT" boxes on your Personal Foundation Chart.

Zap the Tolerations

Key Points

- Having tolerations tends to keep you from growing.
- Every toleration is fixable. Your coach can support you.
- As you fix each one, you lighten up.
- Creating and living a Toleration-Free life is a skill.
- You have better things to do than tolerate.

Introduction

Tolerations are those things that you put up with every day that distract you from other important things. Sometimes the underlying source of continued tolerations is to avoid taking full responsibility for particular circumstances in your life, but eventually you will recognize that this is in large part what is holding you back from achieving your goals. In handling the things you are tolerating, you free up time and energy to devote to a higher quality of life.

Ask Yourself:

- Why do I have tolerations in my life? How do they really work for me?
- Am I ready to find another source of energy? How do I know I am?
- What are alternative positive energy sources?
- What would it mean to have no tolerations, to be a Toleration-Free Zone?

Coaching Tips

○ **Write them down:** It helps to write out all of your tolerations (keep adding to this list), even if you don't know how to resolve the matter. Just putting every toleration on paper is worthwhile. The solution will come.

○ **Look for a pivotal toleration: Pivotal tolerations** refer to something you are putting up with that, when handled, will resolve about five other tolerations, automatically. An example of this is making more money which can be used to fund the replacement of the unreliable car, a housekeeper for the messy house, etc.

○ **Handle the source:** Don't just handle the toleration, make sure you get to and handle the source of it or the problem will reappear, sometimes in a slightly different form. You can **handle the source** of a toleration by eliminating the source, setting up an automatic system, resolving the problem, telling the truth, etc. For example, if you are tolerating living in a city you don't like, don't just change cities, consider the qualities of what environment supports you the best. Then travel the country to really choose the city or area in which you will be most happy, fulfilled and Toleration-Free.

Benefits of Being Toleration-Free

● You stop trying to manage situations that drain your energy and really do not need to be in your way
● You have more energy to devote to your quality of life and to work on the other Coach U Personal Foundation lessons
● You grow more quickly because you are not distracted or weighted down with tolerations
● You are a model for your community as to what is possible for them in this area

10 Steps to a Toleration-Free Life

1. Understand that putting up with things is not useful to anyone.
2. Make a list of 10 things you are tolerating at home.
3. Make the requests and take the actions to eliminate these items.
4. Make a list of 10 things you are tolerating at work.
5. Make the requests and take the actions to eliminate these items.
6. Understand that you are "stunting" your personal growth by tolerating things!
7. Be willing and committed to being Toleration-Free.
8. Stop complaining: instead, make a strong request.
9. Invest $1,000 to handle the tasks/chores that pain you.
10. Do steps 1 through 9 above, again . . . and again . . . if necessary!

Isn't accepting the situation an option.
Don't desires create misery?

Area A: Your Home

Make a list of the five things you are tolerating about your home, whether or not you see a solution to each item. Identify the five items that you are *most* tolerating, whether they are big or small items (limit this now to only five):

1. *House too big*
2. *House needs updating*
3. *New roof*
4.
5.

Personal Foundation Idea Bank

- Geographic location
- Size, style, design of house
- Messes
- Closets unorganized
- Carpet needs shampooing
- Drafts
- Walls need paint
- Appliances need fixing
- Mortgage is too high
- Kitchen, bedroom, etc., is too small
- Furniture is worn

Credit A B C
⦿ ◯ ◯

When you have handled all five tolerations, give yourself credit by coloring in **Area A** of this lesson on the Personal Foundation Chart.

Area B: Your Family/Community

Make a list of the five things you are tolerating about your family or community, whether or not you see a solution to each item. Identify the five items that you are most tolerating, whether they are big or small items (limit this now to only five):

1.
2.
3.

4. _____

5. _____

Personal Foundation Idea Bank

- I need to improve my communication with my spouse
- I need to learn ways to respond and not react to my children
- I have one-way friendships . . . but I tend to stick around anyway
- Spark is missing with spouse, friends
- Neighbors are different and I don't get along with them

Credit A B C ◯ ● ◯   When you have handled all five tolerations, give yourself credit by coloring in **Area B** of this lesson on the Personal Foundation Chart.

Area C: Your Work Life

Make a list of the five things you are tolerating about your work or professional life, whether or not you see a solution to each item. Identify the five items that you are most tolerating, whether they are big or small items (limit this now to only five):

1. _Finances disorganized_

2. _Sometimes lack motivation_

3. _____

4. _____

5. _____

Personal Foundation Idea Bank

- Working for a tough boss
- In the wrong line of work
- Stressed out
- Inadequate pay
- Unpredictable future
- Wrong industry/field
- Inadequate training
- Need more education

Credit A B C ◯ ◯ ●   When you have handled all five tolerations, give yourself credit by coloring in **Area C** of this lesson on the Personal Foundation Chart.

Congratulations! You have just begun to strengthen the foundational skill of reducing tolerations. This skill gets stronger and easier to use the more you recognize how much you are putting up with, and then grow into how little you are willing to put up with. The key here is to continue to tolerate less and less and be able to afford the consequences of this Toleration-Free lifestyle.

Several other lessons found in subsequent modules will develop this skill while using other tools such as Boundaries, Needs, Standards, Clearing, and Values. As you work on these lessons, you will naturally prevent tolerations from occurring around you and be able to immediately handle them when you do.

Get Yourself Clear of the Past

Key Points

- Handle unresolved matters and finish outstanding projects
- It's normal to have unresolved matters and incomplete projects
- You can clear up everything
- Getting clear relies 100% on you
- Getting clear is a skill
- With no unresolved matters, we have more time, space and energy to create a powerful present and outstanding future

Introduction

Getting yourself clear of the past means you are addressing previously unresolved matters such as bad habits or coping skills, an incomplete project, or even unkind remarks that linger as a form of truth for you today. You have several options for getting clear while recognizing that the ultimate goal is to handle new situations as they occur. Like tolerations, the major benefit is the emotional freedom you create to devote to your quality of life.

Having unresolved issues is common. Life moves so fast we tend to move on without completing things. Completing projects, circumstances and relationship issues frees us to be clear in the "here and now."

Ask Yourself:

- What situations cause you to have unresolved matters?
- Why do you let yourself have unresolved matters? Where do you stop? Why do you stop there?
- What would it be like to be fully clear of unresolved matters? What would motivate your actions and life?
- How much of your life is based on what you are not clear of?
- What is the primary source of your unresolved matters?
- What needs to happen to handle the source?
- How far do you currently go to do the maximum in work? Where do you stop? Why? What does complete look like?

Coaching Tips

Start on Coach U's Clean Sweep Program

Begin getting clear of the past by starting on the Clean Sweep program—go for at least 20 points. With the extra burst of energy you get from completing items:

- Look for the source of your unresolved matters—which one(s) of the four areas is "causing" your recurring unresolved matters?
- Get coaching (or counseling) to handle them fully.
- Go back to finishing up Coach U's Clean Sweep program.

It is permissible to complete the Coach U's Clean Sweep program before fully addressing the source of your recurring unresolved matters, but usually the person keeps adding new things to get clear of and never gets the sense of freedom which is possible with the program.

Be Thorough

Rather than take the approach of just getting something done, make sure everything you say, touch, or do is done so thoroughly that nothing about it or the situation will recur for at least five years. Contributing factors to being thorough are:

○ **Being meticulous**
When you clean the car, do you wash everything—the carpet, the underside, the inside of the glove box? Do you change the oil every 3,000 miles?

○ **Excellence**
When you clean the car, do you use the best cleaner available? Do you keep working at it until it shines? Do you use high-grade oil and gas?

○ **Permanence**
When you wash the outside of the car, do you put on a protective coating that will last six months or a year? Is your undercarriage coated to protect from long-term problems like rust? Are you doing everything you can to eliminate all possible problems with your car?

Benefits of Getting Clear of the Past

Few people have a strong enough desire to eliminate all possible future problems. They feel they can handle problems when they arise—and they do; but it is not necessary. In fact, the person who does the maximum advance work in this area has several benefits:

● More Confidence
When you know you've gone the extra mile in one area (like taking great care of your car) it translates to more confidence in every area of your life

● More Time
While the maximum in work does take more initial time, it saves time over the long term .

● Fewer Problems
And you'll get off track less, trying to fix them

● More Opportunities
When you take extraordinary care of what you already have, you are more likely to attract more opportunities

Area A: Clean Sweep Program

Take the 100-question Clean Sweep program checklist, included in the personal foundation program, and access this module in the Resource Section.

Credit **A** B C
◉ ○ ○

When you have answered each of the 100 statements honestly, give yourself credit by filling in **Section A** of this lesson on the Personal Foundation Chart.

Area B: Increase your Clean Sweep score by 20 points

Credit A **B** C
○ ◉ ○

When you have increased your score on the Coach U's Clean Sweep program by 20 points, give yourself credit by filling in **Section B** of this lesson on the Personal Foundation Chart.

Area C: Reach 95 on the Clean Sweep Program

Credit A B **C**
○ ○ ◉

When you have reached a score of 95 on the Clean Sweep program, give yourself credit by filling in **Section C** of this lesson on the Personal Foundation Chart.

Create and Use 10 Daily Habits

Key Points

- Only choose habits you want to do.
- Choose habits that give you energy.
- Have fun with your habits.
- Modify your habits as you wish.
- Never select things that you "should" do.
- Keep your habits simple.

Introduction

There is a daily routine that will keep you focused, clear, motivated and moving forward. We call this routine the 10 Daily Habits. These are the things you do each day, which support the positive changes in your behavior and are foundational to the fundamental shifts that will dramatically improve your life.

Ask Yourself:

- What are the habits that would enrich my experience of life, every day?
- What habits do I tend to continually put on my list but not keep?
- What habits have I been successful at maintaining and what impact have they had on my life overall?

Coaching Tips

○ **Choose habits you want to do.**
There is no place for "shoulds" or "coulds" in your 10 daily habits. Instead, select or design daily habits that you look forward to and give you pleasure, but that you normally would forget to do much of the time without this type of focus.

○ **Choose habits that give you energy.**
Most of the 10 Daily Habits that actually work for people are the ones that add to the person's well-being or energy flow. It might mean that you do something like having five vegetables each day, or that you stop something such as watching television or eating after 7 p.m. We find that a 2:1 ratio of doing and stopping works pretty well.

○ **Modify your 10 Daily Habits, as needed.**
It takes some fine-tuning to have the 10 habits that work best for you. If you find yourself not doing one or two of your habits, change or replace them with ones that come naturally.

○ **Use visual help.**
If you are inspired or motivated by visual reminders, set up a visual display to track your 10 habits each day, similar to the chart on the following page.

My 10 Daily Habits									
Habit		Day 1	Day 2	Day 3	Day 4	Day 5	Day 6	Day 7	Day 8
1.	Floss								
2.	No TV								
3.	Read								
4.	Add Value								
5.	Bike Ride								
6.	Rest								
7.	Veggies								
8.	Love								
9.	Nails								
10.	Simplify								

Benefits of Your 10 Daily Habits

- You have a healthy routine.
- You have a focus.
- You have more energy.
- You are more likely to maintain balance.
- You feel good.

Area A: Create Your 10 Daily Habits

Make a list of the 20 daily habits that you *could* form. Then scale it down to 10 and create a visual display or tracking system to support you in doing these each day.

1. _____

2. _____

3. _____

4. _____

5. _____

6. _____

7. _____

8. _____

9. _____

10. _____

11. _____

12. _____

13. _____

14. _____

15. _____

16. _____

17. _____

18. _____

19. _____

20. _____

Personal Foundation Idea Bank

- Thank one person a day.
- Have whole grains or oats for breakfast.
- Watch no television.
- Read something you really want to read.
- Spend an hour with your children.
- Offer to help someone.
- Go the extra mile for a client or customer.
- Drink decaf instead of caffeine.
- Be in bed by 10 p.m.
- Walk three miles each morning.
- Say "No" most of the day.
- Make your bed.
- Go with your intuition at least once each day.
- Meditate for 20 minutes.
- Write in your journal.
- Take a bath with special minerals.
- Take your vitamins.
- Handle one unresolved matter.

Credit   A   B   C
              ●   ○   ○

When you have selected your 10 Daily Habits and have done them ALL for one day, give yourself credit by filling out **Area A** of this lesson on the Personal Foundation Chart.

Area B: A full week of 10 Daily Habits

You can do it!

Credit   A   B   C
              ○   ●   ○

When you have successfully completed your 10 Daily Habits for five days in a row, give yourself credit by filling out **Area B** of this lesson on the Personal Foundation Chart.

Area C: A full month of 10 Daily Habits

Wow. This is tough. Go for it!

Credit   A   B   C
              ○   ○   ●

When you have successfully completed your 10 Daily Habits for an entire month give yourself credit by filling out **Area C** of this lesson on the Personal Foundation Chart.

Congratulations! This shows you are committed to having each day be yours and be all that it can be.

Simplify Your Life Dramatically

Key Points

- We are all too busy. It's contagious.
- When your schedule is too full, you miss out on life.
- For the best results and biggest statement, toss out 50 percent of what you think is important.
- Boredom can be the gatekeeper to peace.
- Growth occurs faster when there is space.
- Maintain a reserve of space.

Introduction

Our lives are too tightly jammed and scheduled with projects, goals, ideas, coulds, shoulds, have to's, commitments, expectations, concerns and obligations. This climate makes it exceedingly challenging to orient your life around your values, or to find peace and fulfillment. Life becomes a constant struggle just to keep up. You've heard about downscaling and simplifying, but that is so much easier said than done. The purpose of this lesson is to actually *do* it. You will be simplifying 10 aspects of your life.

Ask Yourself:

- Is my life too busy? Why?
- Why have I chosen to do so much?
- What am I building and where am I going with my current lifestyle?
- Is there a better future to it?
- Is that future costing me my present?
- What am I missing about myself because of my current lifestyle?

Coaching Tips

- It is helpful to understand that even if you think your life right now is too busy, too hectic, too full, too whatever, your present can be perfect for you. Contentment resides in the present. You have already covered this concept in previous lessons. However, the present can always be improved, especially on the practical level, and that is what this lesson is all about. All of the lessons in the personal foundation course are designed to elevate your well being and advance you further along your path of development. Some lessons are of a more "practical" or physical nature than others, which serve to assist development of other areas. This is one of those lessons. By simplifying your life dramatically, you will find space to grow faster. Your personal development will accelerate as a result of completing this lesson.

- **We need to offer a cautionary statement here.** When you start to simplify your life, expect a reaction from your "systems." Things will start to break, you will get confused, opportunities and people will disappear, your somewhat predictable life will start zig zagging, you may get headaches and perhaps get sick (this is your physical body reacting to the change of style and pace), your priorities will change, you will wonder who you are and what you're doing. But wait—don't panic—it gets better.

○ You can select the pace at which you want to simplify your life. You can do this overnight by tossing out 50 percent of your projects, or you can phase out commitments, shoulds, goals and tasks over a six-month (or even longer) period. We recommend you take dramatic simplification steps just to tell yourself and others this is the track you are now on. If you do this process gradually, you may never create the momentum needed to complete it.

Understanding Simplifying Your Life

You are naturally drawn to keep your life and yourself complicated and busy.
This occurs for several reasons. You were raised with the mentality that working hard is the solution to success. The mind needs something to do, so it directs us to do "stuff" or create situations that keep it busy. Stimulants, like television, caffeine, nicotine and adrenaline, prevent the body from resting and keep it moving. Technology has rapidly increased over the past 50 years, causing everyone to struggle to keep up with the advances in learning, acquisition, and competition.

Much of the media or your own subculture has affected you more than you know.
What you want, how you live, and what's most important often originate from outside influences. The media and other stimulants can have a strangely seductive influence on your subconscious, drawing you into a place you really do not want to be. You end up not being the person managing and creating your life, yet you don't seem to realize this until you simplify.

The simplification process threatens you in many ways.
You may experience physical and emotional symptoms of withdrawal as you slow down and simplify your life. The body, mind, and spirit must go through expected and natural transitions from a life of cramped clutter to a life with space to breathe. This space may seem foreign and uncomfortable at first. Just remember, boredom is not necessarily a bad thing, and it can even be the gateway to peace.

Guiding Principle 9	**People Define Their Own Integrity.** The vigilant development of the fit between calling and conduct creates integrity.

Benefits of Simplifying Your Life

- You will get back in touch with your values, feelings, and spirit, which were simply not available when you were too busy.
- You will start to make different types of choices than those you made "on the run."
- You will begin to practice extreme self-care because you see and feel the costs of not doing so.
- You will, perhaps for the first time, have a sense of space to grow and the peace to enjoy it.

10 Steps to Simplifying Your Life

1. Understand this is a major step. If you are serious about this, you will be making big changes that will have big effects. Are you ready for this?
2. Evaluate your current life honestly. Where is the clutter, and what is eating up your time, your peace of mind, and your energy? Make a list, be specific, and judge the negative value of these things, as well as the positive.
3. You have most likely gained a great deal from your frenzied pursuits over the past years. What are you willing to let go of? What are you not willing to part with? This includes both the material and the immaterial things. Make a list of both.
4. Make a list of how much of your "busy-ness" is composed of shoulds.
5. Make a list of all of your current commitments (all areas, business, family, financial etc.).
6. Make a list of your habits. Which of these drain you and add to the craziness? Which add value? Distinguish them well.
7. Eliminate all tolerations (see the lesson on this subject).
8. Reorganize your schedule to increase efficiency, even if you don't eliminate anything (of course, deleting things is usually the best way).
9. Analyze your current financial situation.
10. Armed with this information, make a solid plan to simplify.

Area A: Cut it Out!

Your job now is to permanently cut out three projects, tasks, responsibilities, shoulds, coulds, wants, goals, habits, or routines that are not necessary. Not necessary means things that are being done in order to get something else (like volunteering in order to get business), things you used to enjoy but have outgrown, and things that you don't think your life should be without even though you have made it this far just fine without them (spouse, Mercedes, publication as an author, size 8/32-inch waist—you get the idea).

Sometimes it is best to pick the goals and projects that you say you are most committed to and can't live without. These are often the real energy drains that masquerade as great needs, goals and desires, but in reality they are just weights of burden. The focus here is simplification so that goals and wants can be attracted to you instead of you thinking you should be creating them. You cannot access the attraction principle until your life is simplified. Don't even try. Even if you did attract it, there is no place to put it.

On the lines provided, list the three big projects that you are now going to permanently eliminate:

1. _____

2. _____

3. _____

Personal Foundation Idea Bank

- Leadership positions in service organizations. These can drain time, space, and energy if you already have a full life.
- Volunteer positions that do not directly benefit you. Redesign your participation.
- Home projects such as fixing things, building a table, etc. Hire these out or do without.
- Professional organizations that do not directly benefit you.
- Social events that no longer fit you.
- Financial goals that have yet to come true.
- Romantic goals that you think you need. You can't create this—it's a product of attraction.
- Roles that you take too seriously, like parenting 30-year-old children or "living for" a spouse.
- Fantasies and unrealistic goals.
- Egocentric goals such as "being somebody," saving the world, making a contribution—it's time to get real.

A B C

Credit ●○○

When you have permanently eliminated your three big drains, give yourself credit by filling in **Area A** of this lesson on the Personal Foundation Chart.

Area B: Time Wasters

This part of the lesson focuses on the time-consuming tasks, activities, and habits that you do not usually think much about but that waste your life away. This requires open and honest evaluation. Go deep.

You will need to arrange to eliminate, delegate, or systematize 12 tasks to complete this area. *(See the "Personal Foundation Idea Bank" following the table provided.)*

Please list the task and the solution in the table provided:

	Identified Time Drains and Solutions	
	Task	**Solution**
1.		
2.		
3.		
4.		
5.		

	Task	Solution
6.		
7.		
8.		
9.		
10.		
11.		
12.		

Personal Foundation Idea Bank

- Get your food delivered; get your cleaning delivered or hire a weekly service.
- Hire someone to come in four hours a week (or as long as needed) to do your filing or administration.
- Have healthy food prepared or delivered to you.
- Hire a housekeeper to clean your house.
- Use Quicken (or other suitable program) to pay bills, or hire a bill-paying service.
- Use a CPA for taxes.
- Hire a therapist instead of trying to resolve emotional problems, willpower issues, etc. (a big time waster).
- Hire a coach instead of trying to make yourself do something.
- Hire a coach instead of thinking, deciding, figuring out, and planning-but-not-doing.
- Go to Alcoholics Anonymous if you have a drinking problem.
- Go to Overeaters Anonymous if you have an eating problem.
- Seek appropriate help for other addictions.
- For study, hire a mentor, trainer, or tutor.
- Do shopping quarterly or hire it out.

Credit A B C

When you have eliminated, delegated, or systematized 12 tasks, give yourself credit by filling in **Area B** of this lesson on the Personal Foundation Chart.

Area C: The To-Do List

We are all familiar with the to-do list. This is a list that keeps on growing, even though you try to reduce the number of items. This is a very important part of this lesson: Your task is to eliminate your personal to-do list. Yes! Obviously, there are times when the to-do list is helpful, especially for work-related issues, but your personal life does not have to revolve around such a list.

Is it possible to stop using a personal to-do list in today's world of the day-timer? Yes, yes, and yes. However, it takes a little effort. Here are some tips.

- Set up a reminder system for birthdays, dinners, social events, and the like. You can use a wall calendar, a birthday book, or an automated reminder system that emails or calls you before important dates.
- When you think of something that you have to do, stop and ask yourself why you have to do it. Maybe you really don't. It usually involves picking something up, making a call, or doing a task, all of which can possibly be handled a different way, including delegating. Instead, buy your birthday cards and presents in big batches, and have someone whose job it is to do errands, make calls, and so forth for you. (You can afford this. And if you can't, then you are under-earning. Use some of the time you will save in the Personal Foundation program to better your skills, job, pay, and life.)
- Tossing out your to-do list completely is often the best way. Start living without it. You can. Much of what you have on your list is great stuff, but it runs you. You have come to rely on its doing that. Stop it. It is better to live your days in the present, by responding to what is next, rather than allowing a to-do list to run your life. There are many ways to keep the important stuff in a remembrance or reminder system, but toss out the to-do list.
- Be creative. Try other methods to accomplish your needed tasks. You will experience some trial and error, but eventually you will settle into a system that works for you without the list.

Take a few moments to think through how you usually accomplish these kinds of tasks. How can you do them differently, without the list controlling you? Get creative and write down some innovative ways you can toss the list and still do all you need to do, but without the burden. Try inventing workable systems for you.

_____

_____

_____

_____

_____

_____

_____

_____ I have successfully accomplished needed tasks without a to-do list for 1 day.

_____ I have successfully accomplished needed tasks without a to-do list for 1 week.

_____ I have successfully accomplished needed tasks without a to-do list for 1 month.

A B **C**

Credit ◯◯●

When you have systematized your to-do's and permanently tossed out your to-do list, give yourself credit by filling in **Area C** of this lesson on the Personal Foundation Chart.

Congratulations! **Do you feel lighter now? Good! That's the idea.** Just make sure that you get used to not having a neverending to-do list and don't bring it back to life!

Clean Sweep Program

Summary

You have more natural energy when you are clear with your environment, health and emotional balance, money and relationships.

The **Clean Sweep** program consists of 100 items which, when completed, give you the vitality and strength you want.

The program can be completed in less than one year.

Instructions

There are 4 steps to completing the Clean Sweep program.

Step 1: **Answer each question.** If true, check the circle. Be rigorous; be a hard grader. If the statement is sometimes or usually true please DO NOT check the circle until the statement is virtually always true for you. (No "credit" until it is really true!) If the statement does not apply to you or will never be true for you, check the circle. (You get "credit" for it because it does not apply or will never happen.) And, you may change any statement to fit your situation better.

Step 2: **Summarize each section.** Add up the number of checked circles for each of the four sections and write those amounts where indicated.

Step 3: **Color in the checklist on the next page.** Always start from the bottom up. The goal is to have the entire chart filled in. In the meantime, you will have a current picture of how you are doing in each of the four areas.

Step 4: **Keep playing until all boxes are filled in.** You can do it! This process may take 30 or 360 days, but you can achieve a Clean Sweep! Use your coach or a friend to assist you. And check back once a year for maintenance.

Clean Sweep Program 100-Point Checklist

		Sections		
#	A	B	C	D
25				
24				
23				
22				
21				
20				
19				
18				
17				
16				
15				
14				
13				
12				
11				
10				
9				
8				
7				
6				
5				
4				
3				
2				
1				

Give yourself credit as you get points from the 100-point program. Fill in columns from the bottom up.

A. Physical Environment
Number of circles checked (25 max.) _____

○ My personal files, papers, and receipts are neatly filed away.

○ My car is in excellent condition. (Doesn't need mechanical work, repairs, cleaning, or replacing)

○ My home is neat and clean. (Vacuumed, closets clean, desks and tables clear, furniture in good repair; windows clean)

○ My appliances, machinery, and equipment work well. (Refrigerator, toaster, snowblower, water heater, toys)

○ My clothes are all pressed, clean and make me look great. (No wrinkles, baskets of laundry, torn, out-of-date, or ill-fitting clothes)

○ My plants and animals are healthy. (Fed, watered, getting light and love)

○ My bed/bedroom lets me have the best sleep possible. (Firm bed, light, air)

○ I live in a home/apartment that I love.

○ I surround myself with beautiful things.

○ I live in the geographic area I choose.

○ There is ample and healthy light around me.

○ I consistently have adequate time, space, and freedom in my life.

○ I am not damaged by my environment.

○ I am not tolerating anything about my home or work environment.

○ My work environment is productive and inspiring. (Synergistic, ample tools and resources; no undue pressure)

○ I recycle.

○ I use non ozone-depleting products.

○ My hair is the way I want it.

○ I surround myself with music, which makes my life more enjoyable.

○ My bed is made daily.

○ I don't injure myself, or bump into things.

○ People feel comfortable in my home.

○ I drink purified water.

○ I have nothing around the house or in storage that I do not need.

○ I am consistently early or easily on time.

B. Health & Emotional Balance
Number of circles checked (25 max.) _____

○ I use caffeine (chocolate, coffee, colas, tea) less than 3 times per week, total.

○ I rarely eat sugar. (Less than 3 times per week.)

○ I rarely watch television. (Less than 5 hours per week)

○ I rarely drink alcohol. (Less than 2 drinks per week)

○ My teeth and gums are healthy. (Have seen dentist in last 6 months)

○ My cholesterol count is healthful.

○ My blood pressure is healthful.

○ I have had a complete physical exam in the past three years.

○ I do not smoke tobacco or other substances.

○ I do not use illegal drugs or misuse prescribed medications.

○ I have had a complete eye exam within the past two years. (Glaucoma check, vision test)

○ My weight is within my ideal range.

○ My nails are healthy and attractive.

○ I don't rush or use adrenaline to get the job done.

○ I have a rewarding life beyond my work or profession.

○ I have something to look forward to virtually every day.

○ I have no habits that I find to be unacceptable.

○ I am aware of the physical or emotional problems or conditions I have, and I am now fully taking care of all of them.

○ I consistently take evenings, weekends, and holidays off and take at least two weeks of vacation each year.

○ I have been tested for any life-threatening illness for which I am at risk.

○ I use well-made sunglasses.

○ I do not suffer.

○ I floss daily.

○ I walk or exercise at least three times per week.

○ I hear well.

C. Money
Number of circles checked (25 max.) _____

○ I currently save at least 10% of my income.

○ I pay my bills on time, virtually always.

○ My income source/revenue base is stable and predictable.

○ I know how much I must have to be minimally financially independent and I have a plan to get there.

○ I have returned or made-good-on any money I borrowed.

○ I have written agreements and am current with payments to individuals or companies to whom I owe money.

○ I have six months' living expenses in a money market-type account.

○ I live on a weekly budget that allows me to save and not suffer.

○ All my tax returns have been filed and all my taxes have been paid.

○ I currently live well, within my means.

○ I have excellent medical insurance.

○ My assets (car, home, possessions, treasures) are well insured.

○ I have a financial plan for the next year.

○ I have no legal clouds hanging over me.

○ My will is up-to-date and accurate.

○ Any parking tickets, alimony, or child support is paid and current.

○ My investments do not keep me awake at night.

○ I know how much I am worth.

○ I am on a career/professional/business track that is or will soon be financially and personally rewarding.

○ My earnings are commensurate with the effort I put into my job.

○ I have no "loose ends" at work.

○ I am in relationship with people who can assist in my career/professional development.

○ I rarely miss work due to illness.

○ I am putting aside enough money each month to reach financial independence.

○ My earnings outpace inflation, consistently.

D. Relationships
Number of circles checked (25 max.) _____

○ I have told my parents, in the last three months, that I love them.

○ I get along well with my sibling(s).

○ I get along well with my co-workers/clients.

○ I get along well with my manager/staff.

○ There is no one who I would dread or feel uncomfortable "running across". (In the street, at an airport or party)

○ I put people first and results second.

○ I have let go of the relationships that drag me down or damage me. ("Let go" means to end, walk away from, state, handle, no longer be attached to)

○ I have communicated or attempted to communicate with everyone who I have damaged, injured, or seriously disturbed, even if it wasn't fully my fault.

○ I do not gossip or talk about others.

○ I have a circle of friends/family who love and appreciate me for who I am, more than just what I do for them.

○ I tell people how they can satisfy me.

○ I am fully caught up with letters and calls.

○ I always tell the truth, no matter what.

○ I receive enough love from people around me to feel good.

○ I have fully forgiven those people who have hurt/damaged me, deliberate or not.

○ I am a person of his/her word; people can count on me.

○ I quickly clear miscommunications and misunderstandings when they do occur.

○ I live life on my terms, not by the rules or preferences of others.

○ There is nothing unresolved with past loves or spouses.

○ I am in tune with my wants and needs and get them taken care of.

○ I do not judge or criticize others.

○ I do not "take personally" the things that people say to me.

○ I have a best friend or soul mate.

○ I state requirements rather than complain.

○ I spend time with people who don't try to change me.

Benefits

On the lines below, jot down specific benefits, results and shifts that happen in your life because you handled an item in the Clean Sweep program.

Date/Benefit

Intellectual Property Notice

This material and these concepts are the intellectual property of Coach U, Inc. You may not repackage or resell this program without express written authorization and royalty payment. The exception is that you may deliver this program to single individuals without authorization or fee. If you lead a workshop, develop, or deliver a program to a group or company based on or including this material or these concepts, authorization and fees are required. You may make as many copies of this program as you wish, as long as you make no changes or deletions of any kind.

Resources

Attention Readers:

Thank you for participating in the collective wisdom of Coach U. Together, we all continue to learn. Additional resources and forms can be found in the *Coach U's Essential Coaching Tools: Your Complete Practice Resource* book by Coach U, Inc.

Attention CoachInc.com Students and Graduates:

CoachInc.com students and graduates may find additional and/or more recent resources associated with this module in the resource area of the student-only website. If you are a student or graduate of one of CoachInc.com's ICF-accredited coach training programs, you can access these by searching under the name of the course. When the course description page appears you may find a link to the list of additional resources. Each item is a live link to its actual location on the website. Click on the item to access the information.

Do remember to take the associated online self-test for this module once you have completed the course in-person or by TeleClass. The tests are required for coach certification with the International Coach Federation. Throughout the course or anytime you find valuable resources for a particular course, please feel free to add to the value of our curriculum by forwarding the resource to revampteam@coachu.com.

www.coachinc.com

Personal Foundation
Level 2

Overview

○ Benefits Go to Page > 69

By fully participating in the material offered in this module, you will be significantly strengthening and improving your personal foundation through work on the *Who* component.

○ Definitions Go to Page > 70

Please refer to the Definitions section of the Introduction to Personal Foundation module.

○ Concepts Go to Page > 71

What Is Personal Foundation?: The *Who* Component
Your personal foundation is your structural basis that supports you in living an exceptional life. We have called this second part the *Who* of personal foundation, as it defines and discusses who a person is, from the inside out.

○ Distinctions Go to Page > 73

No Distinctions are provided with this module.

○ Application Go to Page > 74

The Application section of each personal foundation module contain the lessons that are the personal application and learning for developing a strong foundation. This module contains eight lessons relating to the *Who* component of personal foundation.

Restore Your Integrity: Integrity refers to how our personal life system is set up and whether or not it works easily and effortlessly, or with great struggle.

Get Your Needs Met: Every person has a specific set of personal needs they must meet. The purpose of this lesson is to identify your specific needs and get them met, once and for all.

Extend Your Boundaries: Boundaries are imaginary lines that you draw around yourself to define the area that is necessary for you to fully express all of yourself.

Raise Your Standards: Personal standards refer to the behavior and actions to which you are willing to hold yourself accountable.

Strengthen Your Family: Harmony, love, and relating on a consistent and interdevelopmental basis are hallmarks of the model family, and can be grown and developed.

Deepen Your Community: People with similar interests and styles get together and stay together and eventually bond together, forming personal communities.

Be Well Protected: When fear of loss is reduced and even eliminated, you will naturally progress. The purpose of this lesson is to offer you safety.

Become a Problem-Free Zone: It helps to understand where problems come from, what fixes them permanently, and what prevents problems so you can enjoy the comfort and lifestyle of being a problem-free zone.

○ Needless Program Go to Page > 120

○ Resources Go to Page > 127

Benefits

By fully participating in the material offered in this module, you will be significantly strengthening and improving your personal foundation through work on the *Who* component of this foundation. You will learn how to be more of the real you.

This module is designed to allow you to:

○ **Work** through eight lessons that will dramatically affect the *Who* of your personal foundation—what we call the real you

○ **Discover** how you can significantly restore your integrity—the wholeness of *Who* you are

○ **Establish** systems, standards, and boundaries that keep you free of problems

○ **Know** exactly *Who* you are in order to live the life you want to live

○ **Do** the groundwork necessary in order to move on to the lessons found in the Personal Foundation Level 3 module, which deal with the *How* of personal foundation

Definitions

Please refer to the Definitions section of the Introduction to Personal Foundation module.

Concepts

What is Personal Foundation?: The *Who* Component

Your personal foundation is your structural basis that supports you in living an exceptional life. Just as a house must be built on a strong foundation to avoid collapsing under stress, so must your life. A house's foundation is made up of earth, cement, and steel. Your personal foundation is also made up of three major elements.

Humans are complex creatures. Volumes have been written about the various components, physical and otherwise, that comprise an individual. Essentially, however, all that we are can be summed up in three parts we often call body, mind, and spirit. To simplify the understanding of these parts, and ultimately the refining and growth of the whole, this personal foundation program will label them the *What, Who,* and *How* of every person.

This module contains lessons relating to the *Who* of personal foundation.

The *Who*

The *Who* part of you is easily understood as the real you, the core of who you are in reality, not in presentation of the *What.* The *Who* often drives the *What,* but is not always consistent with it. The ultimate goal of this program is to bring these parts into efficient and natural alignment. The *Who* can also be identified with the "spirit" part of the body, mind and spirit analogy. It is the source of everything else about you, and corresponds to the source side of the Five-S Model referenced in the previous section. The *Who* contains your being, your source for all else, your place of personal awareness. All shifts and solutions begin at the *Who* of you.

> **❝** You are only young once, but you can stay immature indefinitely. **❞** | **Unknown**

We all reach a place in life where we think the *Who* is stable, unchanging, and static. In reality, however, this essence core is always subject to growth, refinement, spiraling upward (or downward) movement, and awareness. We often think that this seemingly stable core is not in need of attention. On the contrary: personal development means a continuing vigilance to the development and "care and feeding" of the *Who.* It means cleaning out closets and refreshing the air regularly, opening windows of new light and sources of warmth. What we call our "personality" is rooted in the *Who* of us. As the *Who* grows and changes, so does the personality and the *What* that others see. Our personal integrity dwells within the *Who*. It can be neglected, and life's weeds will choke it off. Or it can be carefully tended to flourish into a *What* that is highly attractive to the world.

The Application section of this module contains the lessons pertaining to the *Who* of the personal foundation and includes:

- Restore Your Integrity
- Get Your Needs Met
- Extend Your Boundaries
- Raise Your Standards
- Strengthen Your Family
- Deepen Your Community
- Be Well Protected
- Become a Problem-Free Zone

Distinctions

Because of the somewhat different nature of the contents of the personal foundation modules, no "Distinctions" are provided here. The lessons contained in the "Application" section of each of the four personal foundation modules are relatively self-contained and self-explanatory.

Application

This section is composed of eight different lessons:

- Restore Your Integrity
- Get Your Needs Met
- Extend Your Boundaries
- Raise Your Standards
- Strengthen Your Family
- Deepen Your Community
- Be Well Protected
- Become a Problem-Free Zone

Work your way through all eight lessons and be sure to color in the appropriate "Credit" boxes on your Personal Foundation Chart.

Restore Your Integrity

Key Points

- You are either in integrity or you are not.
- If you are out of integrity, you pay a price.
- Each of us needs our own degree or level of integrity.
- Integrity refers to what makes you whole.
- Being "in integrity" is always a choice.

Introduction

In the building trade, integrity refers to the integration of the bricks, mortar, foundation, plumbing, interlocking pieces, and strength of materials. When it is built and assembled properly, the building has integrity and does not require propping up or much attention, other than maintenance. It can weather almost any storm since it was built properly and well sited.

Integrity in humans refers to how our personal life system is set up and whether it works easily and effortlessly or with great struggle. Without enough integrity, we spend much of our time propping ourselves up, which is costly and distracting.

When "In Integrity"

- One has fewer problems.
- Consistent feelings of peace and well-being are present.
- One reacts to others very little.
- Decisions and choices are clear and easy.

When "Out Of Integrity"

- Disturbances occur regularly.
- Others are blamed, criticized.
- We "react" rather than "respond" to others.
- Decisions and choices are difficult, without clarity.

To be our best, we must be whole: that is, be responsible for our actions and inactions, respond fully to the lessons being offered to us,
honor our bodies and ourselves, and respect the realities of the physical universe.

Ask Yourself:

- What is integrity—to you?
- Are you "in integrity" right now?
- If not, why not?
- How much integrity do you need?
- Has it changed over the last five years?
- What happens if you don't get enough?
- What happens when you do?

Coaching Tips

○ Being in integrity is a personal choice. It is not necessarily about morals but about having the right amount of wholeness in your life. Integrity is not about comparing oneself to others but about being comfortable in your own integrity. Each person defines his or her own level of integrity, and chooses to live within that definition.

○ Integrity is about being whole, where all the pieces of your life fit together easily and are integrated into an unhindered freedom allowing you to be the real person you are.

Understanding Integrity

Integrity is a measure of personal wholeness. It describes how well your actions align with your core values and represent your purpose. As guiding principle #9 tells us, people define their own integrity. You define your level of integrity by vigilantly developing the fit between calling and conduct.

Integrity is the word we use to describe a state of wholeness.
For example, when a skyscraper is built on a strong foundation with plenty of steel beams and high-grade materials to withstand virtually any calamity, we say it is a structure with integrity—all the parts and pieces necessary to preserve its integrity (wholeness) are intact. When a person lives easily and perfectly, and all they do is in harmony with who they really are, the person is "in" integrity.

There is another element to the understanding of integrity. The first definition in the dictionary for this word is "uncompromising adherence to moral and ethical principles; soundness of moral character; honesty." The second definition is "the state of being whole or entire." At first glance, these two definitions may seem completely different. However, being whole does involve the element of adhering to principles. We will not undertake a discussion of the moral and ethical issues surrounding these concepts, but it is healthy to understand that a person's integrity most definitely involves "soundness of moral character" as the dictionary states. For the purposes of this module, we will limit our discussion to the element of personal wholeness.

Guiding Principle 9 | **People Define Their Own Integrity.**
The vigilant development of the fit between calling and conduct creates integrity.

Integrity is Dynamic

Integrity is not a state you try to achieve but a reflection of who you are in any moment, and the dynamic relationship you maintain between purpose and path. As you progress through these lessons to build a stronger personal foundation, you will also find your integrity increasing. Your wholeness is based on a strong personal foundation made up of many parts working in harmony.

"Self" Work and "Integrity" Work

"Self" work involves increasing your awareness of how you interact with yourself, others, and circumstance—mostly on an external basis. The objective is to see yourself reflected in many multifaceted ways and dimensions in order to increase your "self" knowledge and awareness and to strengthen your relationship with yourself. The "integrity" work of personal foundation begins to look at the alignment between who you are and the behavior you engage in. Integrity work allows you to make the shift from operating from an automatic-pilot, reactive state of decision making to a well-thought-out and well-explored plan, based on what really creates your uniqueness in the world and serves you the best.

Personal Levels of Integrity

Everyone has a unique degree of integrity required to be who he or she is intended to be. We are all at different points along the path of development. There are distinct integrity requirements at each point that permit us to grow to the next one. And until we are living in the integrity required to be at any given place on that path, we will not grow to the next place. We begin to see that all of life gets easier as we move along, and the integrity levels will naturally increase.

The Integrity Equation

Integrity is the result of having the following conditions in life:

- No unresolved matters
- Alignment
- Responsibility

Each of these are discussed in various lessons, but you should be aware of them now. Briefly, you are in integrity when:

1. You are clear of the past and in the present.

That is, you have corrected any wrongs, fully communicated any censorships, holding back or disturbances with another, made personal changes to make sure life works well and fully handled every task and job.

2. Your life is aligned and balanced.

That is, your goals are aligned with your True Values, your actions are based on what is true, not a fantasy or delusion, and your commitments are aligned with your vision or purpose. Your life is aligned with something bigger than your ego.

3. You are responsible for all that occurs in your life.

This does not mean responsible as in to be blamed for having caused the problems—rather, responsible as in handling whatever occurs and then making necessary adjustments so this type of problem does not occur again. Being responsible does not mean complaining; it means handling and resolving.

Benefits of Being in Integrity

- You will have more energy and an effortlessness about achieving the results you want.
- You will consistently attract appropriate and fulfilling people in your life who are reliable, empowering, loving, and inspiring.
- Restoring and being in integrity is a process that adds richness to your life—enjoy it.

10 Steps to Restoring Integrity and Wholeness

1. Make a list of 10 ways you are currently not in integrity.
2. Get to the source of each and every item; resolve all fully.
3. Make a commitment to start living in integrity, as you see it.
4. Let go of at least 10 "shoulds, coulds, woulds, oughts, wills."
5. Involve a coach or other strong, able person to help you.
6. Start getting 50 percent more reserve than you feel you need.
7. Utilize additional Coach U resources.
8. Stop hanging out with people who are not the best models.
9. Eliminate adrenaline and other unhealthy "rushes" in your life.
10. Let go of everything you know is not good for you.

Area A: Choosing Integrity

Please respond to the following set of questions and statements.

Where is my life "in integrity" now?

1. _____

2. _____

3. _____

4. _____

5. _____

Where is my life "not in integrity" now, and how do I know this?

1. _____

2. _____

3. _____

4. _____

5. _____

What are the five big (or small) changes that I would need to make that are pivotal enough to restore the integrity in all five areas? Be big and creative.

1. _____

2. _____

3. _____

4. _____

5. _____

What would I lose by restoring my integrity, specifically? By *lose,* we mean what loss would you feel if you made the switch? (Hint: often the areas or things we are out of integrity about feed us energy, make us right, give us something to do. In other words, it sometimes works for us to be out of integrity, at least for now.)

1. _____

2. _____

3. _____

4. _____

5. _____

If you have chosen integrity, why have you? And how do you know?

1. _____

2. _____

3. _____

4. _____

5. _____

A B C

Credit ● ○ ○

When you have answered these questions thoroughly and honestly, give yourself credit by filling in **Area A** of this lesson on the Personal Foundation Chart.

Area B: Restoring Integrity

There are things that you are out of integrity in—things that are hurting you or holding you back, people or places you are hiding behind, systems that are missing, things you are doing that just don't work, etc.

In the space that follows, identify 10 specific items, actions, habits, or activities that you know keep you out of integrity. You may pull from the information in Area A or create a new list. Next to each item, write down the specific solution in one or two words. Keep it simple and make it an action—something you can do versus something you need to wait to occur (conditional actions).

These are highly specialized areas of focus, and may require some specialist knowledge in each field. CoachInc.com training programs offer a number of courses that provide appropriate training in these areas.

Item Out of Integrity	Action/Solution
1. _____	_____
2. _____	_____
3. _____	_____
4. _____	_____
5. _____	_____
6. _____	_____
7. _____	_____
8. _____	_____
9. _____	_____
10. _____	_____
11. _____	_____
12. _____	_____

Personal Foundation Idea Bank

- Working at the wrong job
- Spending time with a community that does not bring out your best
- Having extramarital affairs
- Putting yourself at undue physical risk
- Living in an environmentally toxic area
- Living in fear
- Living in debt
- Misrepresenting yourself
- Over-promising results
- Usng addictive substances or engaging in compulsive behavior

Credit A B C ○ ● ○ When you have systematized your to-do's and tossed out your to-do list, give yourself credit by filling in **Area B** of this lesson on the Personal Foundation Chart.

Area C: The Big One

Area B has been completed, but now we need to again select/articulate/create one big integrity area or item that, when restored, will change your life so you will never be the same. For many people, there is often something underlying that is being taken for granted as "normal." You should now be able to see what this is given the work you did in Area B. What is it? Please write this down in the area below and identify the three-point solution. If you cannot think of anything, wait; it will come to you in the next month or so as you work on other lessons in this program. Ask your coach for help on developing solutions.

The Big One

_____

_____

_____

The Solution

1. _____

2. _____

3. _____

A B **C**

Credit ○ ○ ● _____

When you have identified and permanently resolved the big one, give yourself credit by filling in **Area C** of this lesson on the Personal Foundation Chart.

Congratulations! Tough one, yes? Good for you. It helps to go this deep, which makes the other lessons more fun and gives them a solid place to reside.

Get Your Needs Met

Key Points

- Personal needs dominate one's life if not met.
- A need must be met; it's not optional.
- When needs are satisfied, we can be ourselves.
- Needs are completely satisfiable.
- If it's not satisfiable, it's an addiction or compulsion.
- Integrity comes first, needs second, wants third.

Introduction

In addition to physical needs such as air, water, shelter and food, every person has a specific set of personal needs they must have met. The purpose of this lesson is for you to identify your specific needs and get them met, once and for all. You will see that identifying and getting your needs met is simply a skill to be mastered. Once you do this, you are able to develop at a much faster pace.

Ask Yourself:

- Do you understand the concept of needs and the driving force behind them?
- What needs do you have in your life right now?
- Have you explored the impact that unmet needs have had in the choices you have made or chosen not to make?
- Are you clear or unclear as to how to meet your needs in a manner that actually begins to satisfy them?

Coaching Tips

- It takes a while to get comfortable with the notion that you can get your needs met permanently.

- Needs change over time. The key here is to master the skill of immediate needs satisfaction so this skill can work for you, behind the scenes, as you live your life.

- It takes time to get your needs satisfied and to set up ways to consistently meet your needs. Be patient. You'll get better and faster at this over time, and working on the other lessons concurrently will help in this area, too.

- Make sure you understand the difference between a need and an addiction or compulsion. A need can be satisfied on a regular basis; an addiction or compulsion cannot. A need is part of who you are—a feature; an addiction or compulsion is a problem, and this process will not work. A 12-step program or therapy usually does.

Understanding Needs

Needs are what run you.

The main idea behind the concept of needs is that humans are fueled by energy obtained through either healthy or unhealthy sources. Some examples of healthy energy sources include love, interactions with other healthy people, and perhaps a higher power. Unhealthy sources of energy include adrenaline, unmet needs, and suffering. Part of being on a spiritual path is learning to harness the healthy energy. This transition (similar to switching from polluting, smelly, and inefficient fossil fuel to clean, natural, and consequence-free solar power) takes time and practice.

In the meantime, a person is run by unmet needs. It is what gets most people up in the morning, why people get married, how they choose a profession or the job they take, how they get motivated, and what brings them together to commiserate and to develop friendships and relationships.

Needs can be satisfied, once they have been identified.

Needs are a temporary phenomenon that most of us turn into a lifetime activity. Needs are not like the fire in the fireplace, which requires the continuous feeding of wood to keep it going, but we often get connected to chasing rather then getting our needs met. Needs can be satisfied to the degree that they no longer run us as long as we create a method to continually keep getting them met, once and for all. This is not an immediate process and can take years of effort and attention. Also, an area where we have a need will always be a bit vulnerable, especially when we are under stress, have an emotional challenge, or have dramatic change in our lives.

Needs are normal and unique.

Most of us are somewhat hesitant if not embarrassed and/or ashamed, when it comes to admitting and discussing our needs. When you realize that needs are not unusual you come to understand that they are not a reflection on your value as a human being. Needs are, in fact, a common aspect of the human condition. When left unmet, needs drive all of us, whether one has identified their needs or not. Needs tend to be generated from some scar from a past experience and are unique to you and that experience. Someone else may have had a similar experience that did not create any sort of impression.

Benefits of Getting Your Needs Met

- You free up a lot of time.
- You can move on and orient your life around your values.
- You will have mastered a skill that will work well for you forever.
- You stop running in circles.
- You start attracting people and opportunities rather than repelling them.

10 Steps to Getting Your Needs Met

1. Identify as many of your needs as possible. Evaluate whether they are really needs and if you can do without these things. For a real eye-opener, ask three other people what they honestly see as your unmet needs.
2. Identify your top four personal needs using Coach U's NeedLess program.
3. Follow the instructions in that program to eliminate or satisfy your top four needs.
4. Understand that personal needs can be fully satisfied, or even eliminated.

5. Set up a selfish automatic sprinkler system (S.A.S.S.—see NeedLess program) for each of your four needs.

6. Understand that you may have to educate others about your needs, especially if they are involved in the satisfaction of those needs. Ultimately, others should not be a source of getting needs met.

7. See the difference between neediness and needs satisfaction.

8. Understand that other people cannot be responsible for meeting your needs. You are responsible for meeting your needs—no one else.

9. Understand the difference between needs, fantasies, wants, desires, and goals. Work to minimize any needs in your life so you can be free to work on the wants and desires.

10. Learn to simplify and be satisfied with the perfect present.

Area A: Pick A Need

Refer to the Resource section for access to Coach U's NeedLess program and read the list of 200 needs and check approximately 10 (more if you wish) that resonate as a need for you. You are looking for a need—not a want, a should, a fantasy, or a wish. A need is a must for you to be your best. Part of the first step is to tell the truth about what you actually need. This may be the first time you have ever admitted this to yourself. Some of these you will know instinctively. Others require more honest appraisal. Please be willing to "try on" words you might normally skip over. These may be hidden needs. If so, you may have one or more of the following reactions:

- "No, no, no; I don't want THAT to be a need!"
- You can't get to the next word quickly enough.
- "If that is true, I'd have to change my life a lot!"
- You flush, blush, or shake when reading the word.

Got the idea? Good. Now check the words (at least 10) you believe to be personal needs. Ask yourself: "If I had this, would I be able to reach my goals and vision without effort?" (Work, yes; but struggle, no.) You will eventually pick only one need to work on at the moment. Don't make it too easy or too hard.

Good. Now pick the *one* you want to work on to get 100 percent satisfied over the next 90 days and enter it here:

My chosen need: _____

Credit

A B C
● ○ ○

When you have selected the need you are going to work with, give yourself credit by filling in **Area A** of this lesson on the Personal Foundation Chart.

Area B: Satisfy the Need

Already? Sure! There are several ways to get needs satisfied.

1. Reduce the need for the need. Having a strong personal foundation in the other areas will naturally upgrade your life and systems so you need less of everything. For example, when your boundaries are more extensive, there are fewer threats, so your need for safety is reduced. When your integrity is restored, the holes are plugged (which often include need holes). And when you get a reserve, you've moved beyond the need phase. So keep working on the other lessons in this program and you will find you have fewer needs.

2. Set up an automatic system to get the need met. The key to an automatic satisfaction system is that it occurs without your having to create it every time, or manage it or rely on yourself. You just want it to be available and to work. What you'll find, as you shamelessly ask for all that you need, is that when you ask about or create the solution, the need itself actually diminishes, because you are bringing it out in the open and including others as your partners. This alone supports fixing the need simply by its being exposed rather than being hidden deep within. It's very difficult to get secret needs met.

3. Including others in getting your needs met is an important step. Most of us use our family or friends to get our needs met, yet few of us have had a direct conversation with them about which needs and how they are getting met. This conversation is important to have. Once you admit your specific needs, you can share them with others and better see how these needs can be met directly and simply. Most people are very willing to meet your needs if you are direct and responsible about it. It's the covert or unconscious behavior that turns people off. A vital note of caution, however: You cannot depend on or look to others to always meet your needs. Ultimately, you are responsible for getting your needs met or eliminating the need altogether. If you have a need that depends solely on the actions, reactions, or attitudes of others, you may need to take an honest look at the need and discover alternative ways of meeting it. Do not depend on others solely to meet your needs. You provide the system that will satisfy them.

Your exercise is to get your need 100% satisfied in 30 days.
Please fill in the following to get started:

1. My chosen need: _____

2. What percent of my time/energy is spent directly or indirectly trying to get this need met? ____%

3. Why do I have this need? What causes it?

a. _____

b. _____

c. _____

4. How big is this need? How much do I need of this need in order for it to be permanently satisfied? What's the measure amount? How much is too much?

a. _____

b. _____

c. _____

5. What are the costs to me of not having this need met? (Financial, emotional, creative, etc.)

a. _____

b. _____

c. _____

6. What are the benefits to me of not having this need met? (Energy, ego, etc.)

a. _____

b. _____

c. _____

Am I ready to get this need met? _____ YES _____ NO

7. What is the best and easiest way to reduce the need for this need?

a. _____

b. _____

c. _____

8. What are the elements of an automatic satisfaction system that would work?

a. _____

b. _____

c. _____

9. Who can help me to meet this need? What do I need for them to do? (Name/assignment)

a. _____

b. _____

c. _____

A B C

Credit ○ ● ○ _____

When you have filled in all of these lines and taken action on items 7, 8, and 9 to the extent that your need is satisfied, give yourself credit by filling in **Area B** of this lesson on the Personal Foundation Chart.

Area C: Post-Need Zone

A post-need zone is when your life is set up so that you have very, very few needs. Actually, you have needs, but they are being met transparently because you set up the right people and satisfaction systems and have reduced what you "need" dramatically, given your work in other areas of this program. You will know when you are here.

Credit   A B **C**   ○○◉ ────────────────────────────────────

When you are NeedLess, give yourself credit by filling in **Area C** of this lesson on the Personal Foundation Chart.

Congratulations! This is usually the most challenging lesson. It's also the one you will feel most proud to have accomplished.

Extend Your Boundaries

Key Points

- Boundaries help you define who you are and who you are not.
- You need boundaries in order *to be,* and to be you.
- You set boundaries by stopping certain behaviors of yourself or others.
- You extend boundaries by having courage.
- You get the courage from being attentive to yourself.

Introduction

Boundaries are imaginary lines that you draw around yourself to define the area that is necessary for you to fully express all of yourself. Without boundaries there is typically not enough room for you to grow, or at best, you are stifled. However, you can learn how to design and implement boundaries so you can manage what is necessary and make the process effortless for you and for others.

Boundaries are about what others cannot do *to* you or *around* you, and how much what they do hinders your space. Boundaries are about the actions of others and the associated influences on you.

With Healthy Boundaries
- Fear diminishes significantly; trust is rarely an issue.
- Willing, healthy family members and true friends respect you more.
- You start growing more, emotionally, developmentally, and spiritually.

With Weak Boundaries

- You attract needy, disrespectful people into your life.
- You waste a lot of energy to keep life going.
- There is often some urgent issue to be dealt with now—the source of the issue is often "personal space."

Ask Yourself:

- How do boundaries work for you?
- Can you go too far in setting boundaries?
- How would you need to come across in order for people to get these boundaries without your having to read them the riot act or be hard or defensive?
- What is the most powerful, yet graceful, way to interact with others about boundaries?

Coaching Tips

○ Set boundaries because you know that you are being held back from growing into your full being by not having the space to do it. You can be very, very graceful when setting boundaries; you needn't wield a machete or have to build walls.

○ Setting boundaries is a skill you can master. At first, you may be clumsy or go too far, but eventually it will be a natural experience.

○ Give the people or situations that you extend your boundaries around a chance to grow with you and learn from you during this process, instead of just announcing your boundaries in a take-it-or-leave-it way. Share what you are learning about boundaries with them and get them up to speed.

○ Setting boundaries is not a way to vent your anger. Often, people who have "taken it" from others for a long time discover the process of setting boundaries and use it as a way to get even with others. Set your boundaries as a way to love yourself, not vent on others.

○ It's also helpful to see that having weak or undefined boundaries can be a source of great friction and energy for you. In fact, you may have learned to do quite well with this type of energy (although it is expensive and toxic). By setting or extending boundaries, you may find that the process reduces the amount of energy you are receiving. In other words, just understand that if you are resisting setting extensive boundaries, you probably are thriving on not having boundaries although you complain about or are hurt by people or situations invading your space. It may take some time to get used to the quieter, subtler, higher-quality energy that is available once your boundaries are extended. Ease into and change yourself enough to be able to live well with this new type of energy.

Understanding Boundaries

Boundaries help to define who you are.

Healthy people set boundaries, which allow plenty of space for them to try on new behaviors, make mistakes, fulfill needs, and bringing *all* of their best forth in its best form. Also, healthy boundaries help you to attract certain people that nourish and celebrate with you. Boundaries are essential to becoming a healthy adult. Your boundaries act as a filter and either permit or not allow certain people, behaviors, or situations to enter your defined "space" to either enhance or limit you. Proper boundaries make the needs satisfaction process much, much easier. Strong boundaries keep abusive, needy, or non-nourishing people at a reasonable distance from you so that you are not drained and can spend your time fulfilling your needs, wants, and desires.

Establish bigger boundaries than you actually need.
Learning how many boundaries to set and how big to make them is a personal experiment. A good strategy is to set much bigger boundaries than you think you need. Give yourself more than enough space. Be greedy, if necessary, and be strong. The people who really care will understand.

Boundaries become automatic.
At some point, your boundaries will be automatic, requiring no attention on your part, and will rarely be tested by others. You will be living a consistent temperament and style that most people will understand and respect—also automatically.

Benefits of Having Extensive Boundaries

- You will attract people who have a similar respect for themselves.
- You will have more room in which to grow because you are not being drained or violated.
- Your standards have room to rise.
- You will eliminate a great deal of fear.

10 Steps to Having Extensive Boundaries

1. Understand that you need to dramatically extend your boundaries.
2. Be willing to educate others on how to respect your new boundaries.
3. Be relentless, yet not punitive, as you extend boundaries.
4. Make a list of the 10 things that people may no longer do around you, do to you or say to you.
5. Sit down with each person involved and share with him or her your process; get their commitment to honoring you.
6. Insist that every person in your life deliver their comments in positive ways. No more digs, make-funs, deprecating remarks, criticisms—no matter what or who or the situation.
7. Have and use a four-step plan of action whenever someone violates your boundaries, such as:
   a. Inform them what they are doing.
   b. Request they stop immediately.
   c. Demand they stop.
   d. Walk away without any sarcastic, nasty, or get-even comments.
8. Make a list of 10 ways you are violating others' boundaries.
9. Stop violating the boundaries on that list.
10. Reward; congratulate those who are respecting your boundaries.

Area A: Your Time

This is very important. The simple solution, of course, is to say "No" about 1,000 times. On the lines provided, identify where your boundaries are weak or where you are permitting others to cross them. Then, next to each one, write in a two-word solution to the problem. Be specific.

Boundary being crossed   **Action/Solution**

1. _____   _____

2. _____   _____

3. _____   _____

4. _____   _____

5. _____   _____

6. _____   _____

7. _____   _____

8. _____   _____

9. _____   _____

10. _____   _____

Personal Foundation Idea Bank

- You are given a new project by your boss that causes you stress.
- You are appointed head of the committee because no one else volunteered (or you volunteered because no one else did).
- Your children use you as a delivery service instead of creating their own solutions.
- You're the one who gets things done, so everyone gives you their stuff to do.
- You're the one people turn to for support, advice, and coaching, even though you're not getting paid for this.
- You say "Yes" when you mean to say "No."
- You say "Yes" when you'd rather say "No," but you want something out of it.

A B C
Credit ● ○ ○

When you have identified the 10 time-boundary problems in your life and have taken strong action on each one for 30 days, give yourself credit by filling in **Area A** of this lesson on the Personal Foundation Chart.

Area B: Your Heart

Humans are sensitive creatures, but we're also pretty hardy. Fortunately, boundaries can be designed to allow us to be sensitive, no matter what. It's this sensitivity that is the source of our loving, caring, support, and connection with others. It is worth protecting and it can be well protected with boundaries. Most people may not intend to be hurtful in things they say or do, but regardless of their intent, we do get hurt, and the result of that hurt ranges from shutting us down to simply making us annoyed. However, it all damages the heart.

These are suggestions of language you can use to extend your boundary of the heart. Feel free to adapt it to your culture and needs, but do be direct and directive.

- "That's hurtful. Please stop."
- "Ouch! Please apologize!"
- "You're not being nice to me. I am nice to you. You need to be nice to me."
- "What you just said is inappropriate."
- "I am a very sensitive person, and I ask that you respect this about me and be careful what you say. I will do the same for you."
- "I've been doing some work on boundaries that will affect our relationship and I want to share with you what is okay and not okay to happen between us."
- "You know how you joke around about . . . ? Well, I recently realized that it hurts me, and I ask you to respect this and to stop doing it. What you can do is . . ."

Now, on the lines provided, write down the five people or situations that are hurting you, even a little bit, and then write in what you are going to say to them in the next three days, not waiting for a reoccurrence.

1. _____   _____

2. _____   _____

3. _____   _____

4. _____   _____

5. _____   _____

A B C

Credit ◯ ⬤ ◯   When you have identified five heart violations and spoken with the person about them, and they have not reoccurred for 30 days, give yourself credit by filling in **Area B** of this lesson on the Personal Foundation Chart.

Area C: Your Spirit

The spirit referenced here is your essence, the heart and soul of who you are. You might also call this your integrity—your wholeness. Here, you decide what you will allow to affect your spirit's well-being and what you will not.

Types of spirit boundaries include:

- Not accepting gossip from others.
- Not letting unaware people take up your space.
- Not engaging in debates or trying to prove your point with others who don't have a clue.
- Not being in environments that damage or diminish your spirit.

On the lines provided, identify the five spirit boundaries that you feel good about drawing or extending:

1. _____

2. _____

3. _____

4. _____

5. _____

Credit   A   B   **C**
◯ ◯ ◉ _____

When you have drawn or extended these boundaries for 30 days, give yourself credit by filling in **Area C** of this lesson on the Personal Foundation Chart.

Congratulations! You now have room to be you and to grow even more quickly.

Raise Your Standards

Key Points

- Your standards are how you have chosen to behave.
- The higher your standards, the better your life.
- Questioning and reinforcing your standards is valuable.
- Match your standards to your personal needs.
- Only set standards that fit right today.

Introduction

Personal standards refer to the behavior and actions to which you are willing to hold yourself accountable. You will find as you work on this lesson that you will much more easily expect (and enjoy) more of yourself, and others as well.

Ask Yourself:
- What are your current standards?
- Are they high enough? Too high?
- How high should your standards go?
- What is the risk to setting high standards? Low standards?
- What is the relationship between standards and needs?

| Guiding Principle **7** | **People Live from Their Perception.**
An inclusive, present-based perception of reality
is the platform for effective action. |

Coaching Tips

○ Standards are healthy when you move easily into them, which means that you are ready for them and they are ready for you. If you raise your standards too soon, they quickly turn into "shoulds." If you push yourself into standards, you have missed the point. You, in a sense, want to attract them to you. You attract by working on other areas of your personal foundation.

○ Declare your new standard when it is obvious that it is now you. Don't declare your new standard until you are really there or at least on the threshold of being there. A gap is fine, but make sure when you are setting standards for yourself that at least one foot has bridged the gap.

○ Standards are what you do for yourself or behavior that you hold yourself to willingly, as distinct from boundaries (what others cannot do to or around you) and requirements (what others must do for or around you).

○ Standards are not affirmations. Affirmations are about creating a future that one is trying to grow into, or statements that one believes will come (or be) true if one says them often enough. Standards are what is already true and you are just now seeing and saying it. There is very little creation with standards; they are more of an articulation of what is already true.

Understanding Personal Standards

Set your standards very high.
Standards are the behaviors and actions that you hold yourself to honoring. Now that you have set boundaries, it is time to look inward and choose who you are by the standards you honor and what you hold yourself accountable to being and doing.

A high personal standard *must be a choice*. You can't decide to establish a high personal standard simply because it will get you something or because you think you *should* have it. Rather, choose a high personal standard because it is and always has been you, although you may not have fully acknowledged it until now.

Examples:
(Super) High personal standards
- Being positive in everything you say or do with another
- Being fully responsible for everything (good or bad) that happens to you or around you

- Allowing others to be right
- Maintaining a reserve level that gives you peace

High personal standards
- Telling the truth and graciously accepting the consequence
- Putting people ahead of results
- Conducting all business and personal activities honestly

Basic personal standards
- Being helpful
- Being nice to the dog
- Paying your bills on time

Match your high personal standards to your needs.

The higher the standard you can honor, the faster your needs disappear. Set high personal standards if you want to move beyond the domain of reacting to your needs. After you have established boundaries and begun getting your needs met, you will have grown enough to start raising your personal standards. When properly set and honored, these standards are big and strong enough to help you transcend needs.

Enjoy your newly raised standards.

Standards are to be enjoyed for the higher quality of life they provide. Standards are not weapons to use against others. They are your personal choice. You may wish others in your family and community to raise their standards, but don't use yours against them or as a way to make yourself feel superior. Standards are a measure of who you are now. Spend time and develop relationships with people whose standards you admire. They will enjoy your newly found level of attractiveness, too.

Benefits of Setting and Raising Standards

- You become a more authentic you.
- Stuff that you don't want stops coming into your life.
- You tolerate fewer distractions, negativity, and time wasters naturally while you develop a greater tolerance for things that are most important.

10 Steps to Raising Personal Standards

1. Make a list of 10 people you admire: identify their qualities, natural behaviors, and how they handle tough situations and people. What standards could you raise that would make you more like them, yet would still fit you, today?
2. Start being unconditionally constructive every time you open your mouth, yet still say all you need to say.
3. Stop gossiping, good or bad, about anyone.
4. Let go of the standards you "should" have; make a list of the 10 standards you most want and are ready for today.
5. Understand that standards are a choice, not a requirement.
6. Fully respond to everything that occurs in your space; assume you had something to do with it, but don't take the blame. Just handle it and raise your standards so it doesn't happen again.
7. Always put people and relationships ahead of results.
8. Always put your integrity first, needs second, wants third.

9. Always honor the standards of others.
10. Always maintain a reserve of time, money, love, and well-being.

Area A: Who You Are

The object here is to articulate a single standard that fully captures who you are as a human being. Examples include:

- I am someone who lives simply.
- I am someone who tolerates nothing.
- I am someone who takes extremely good care of myself.
- I am someone who has no unresolved matters.
- I am someone who is.

Please fill in the following with the truth of who you are as a human being:

I am someone who _____

_____

A B C

Credit ●○○

When you have articulated the "Who" standard and feel strongly that what you have articulated is you (and there is ample evidence to support this), give yourself credit by filling in **Area A** of this lesson on the Personal Foundation Chart.

Area B: How You Relate

The second part of standards is to identify the type of person you are (or are becoming) in terms of how you relate with others and/or your environment. Examples include:

- I am someone who is generous with others.
- I am someone who responds fully to my environment and others.
- I am someone who touches every person I come in contact with.
- I am someone who is responsible for all that occurs around me.

Please fill in the following with the truth of how you now relate:

I am someone who _____

_____

A **B** C

Credit ○●○

When you have articulated the "Relating" standard and feel strongly that what you have articulated is you (and there is ample evidence to support this), give yourself credit by filling in **Area B** of this lesson on the Personal Foundation Chart.

Area C: What You Do (How You Conduct Your Life)

The third area of standards is the "who you are in what you do." In other words, how you live your life, what you do for a living, how you decide what to do, etc. Examples include:

- I am someone who serves others as my calling.
- I am someone whose life is values-based.
- I am someone who is living my life purpose.

Please fill in the following with the truth of what you do or how you conduct your life:

I am someone who _____

_____

A   B   **C**

Credit ◯ ◯ ● _____

When you have articulated the "Living" standard and feel strongly that what you have articulated is you (and there is ample evidence to support this), give yourself credit by filling in **Area C** of this lesson on the Personal Foundation Chart.

Congratulations! It's nice to know *Who* you are, isn't it? This knowledge (and growth) will serve you well.

Strengthen Your Family

Key Points

- Your family is a major part of who you are.
- Your family can be a source of strength for you and each member.
- Your family's past can be freed for a powerful future.
- Families are not perfect but can grow stronger daily.
- Families require constant tending and loving maintenance.
- Families can be one of your most powerful sources of safety and refuge.

Introduction

For the purpose of this lesson, *family* refers to either your biological or your chosen family. The lesson here is that harmony, love, and relating on a consistent and interdevelopmental basis are hallmarks of the model family and can be grown and developed.

Ask Yourself:

- Is my family the support to me now that it could be?
- Am I the support to my family that I could be?
- What areas of my family (communication, honest feedback, genuine caring, etc.) can be strengthened?
- How would I do that, and what would be required?

Coaching Tips

○ **Quite often, over the course of completing this lesson, certain difficult issues will arise that must be confronted honestly.**
Some of those, which initially and commonly surface, have to do with parental issues—our parents. These will naturally affect how you parent your own children or how you view yourself. Work through these issues so that the past is clear and clean.

○ **You didn't choose your parents, and they didn't choose you.**
Accept that the parents that were given to you were given for a purpose and that they created a relationship with you to the best of their ability. Sometimes parents are ahead of the child's wisdom-grace-love curve; sometimes they are hopelessly behind it. Your parents have contributed to your life today, and that was their choice. It is now your choice how you contribute to theirs (if you have that opportunity) and how you accept and use what they have already given you. You can choose to live under a burden of guilt, shame, or blame, or be free of the past so the future is full of possibility.

○ **How do I resolve the problem of the parent (or other person) who treated me poorly or didn't raise me well?**
You come to a place of acceptance that they did the best they could at the time and you find it in your heart to forgive them. It may help to place full responsibility on the parent(s) who hurt you or who didn't do a good job—in your opinion. Yes, perhaps they blew it. Perhaps they should have done much, much better. And quite possibly they would if they had a chance to do it over again. Tell the parent exactly what they did and didn't do that harmed you and caused damage—but do it with love. You need to speak your truth. Whether they accept the responsibility is up to them. Your objective is not to blame them, make them wrong, or make them agree with you. Your only point is to say what needs to be said about what the truth is for you; their reaction, acceptance or denial, is moot. If you need them to admit to, agree with, or validate your communication or assertions, then you are either trying to get even or don't have enough self-confidence to believe what you believe. You may need to grow into this confidence, but it starts when you place responsibility where it belongs, untangle the past, and make the relationship with your parents a real choice. Forgiveness comes from you first, even if your parents don't ask for it. Lack of forgiveness will become a stumbling block, a great impediment, and an actual burden on your path of development. Let it go.

○ **I continue to have a difficult time with my parents, my spouse, my children (or others).**
Use what you have learned in the personal foundation program and establish extensive boundaries. Examine honestly your interdevelopmental communication to determine whether you are feeding from unhealthy connections. This may be a hidden need for you that requires elimination, perhaps through professional resources.

○ **Acknowledge any potential need for professional therapy.**
Some wounds and situations (past or present) need the help of outside professionals, trained therapists who can work with you to heal those wounds so you can grow beyond them to live a loving, fulfilling life. Be honest about those areas, which may require this kind of assistance. Don't blame, don't hesitate, don't deny. Take care of any past or current dysfunctions and wounds that need to be healed. Do it now.

Understanding Strengthening the Family

A family is a vital source of support, safety, and comfort. You can't do without it.
One of the traditional roles of the family has been a source and structure of safety, security, nurturing, and identity for all members of the family, young and old. If the family is only a place for training and does not offer a reserve of safety and comfort for all members, something very important is missing. Sometimes these missing factors require professional help. Be alert to these situations and deal with them openly. Sometimes people, especially hurting people, make the mistake of thinking they can survive without the supporting family structure. While this may appear possible with some people, in reality all they end up doing is replacing this missing vital component with something else, which may or may not be healthy for them. There is always a hole where the family should be. Families can be healed and made whole if the members are willing to commit to that healing process. Don't abandon it lightly. Realize that your family is vital to you, and you to them. The family, whether strong or weak, will perhaps play the most important part of our development, as both children and adults. Commit to making every effort to strengthen it.

Guiding Principle 1 | **People Have Something in Common.**
We return to the common ground of being by loving, honoring, and valuing self and others.

Families can, and should, grow interdevelopmentally.
A family is not intended to be a dictatorship where members are not allowed a voice or an opinion. While an authority structure is necessary and vital to the growth of children, the family can act as a partnership for each other's growth. Children learn from and model their parents, but parents can also learn from their children if they are open to such learning. Protection, guidance, and development are parental roles, but children can be encouraged to learn and practice this behavior with other family members. Instead of featuring only top-down development, families should be a place for interdevelopment where all members benefit from all others. Sometimes this takes work and practice and encouragement. Unfortunately, our world today sometimes seems a little cold and lacking in respect and genuine interdevelopmental opportunities. If these are taught and cultured within the family, the world is automatically affected positively.

Families today are in a state of constant change.
We have to face the reality of current statistics that tell us that "whole" families are rare. Many of today's families consist of parts of the original whole, blended families, and remnants of what once was. Perhaps our concept of family is changing, but our understanding of the need for family strength, no matter what the consistency, should not. If anything, we should be more committed to the time, process, and energy required to maintain family structure and even strengthen it. The need for a safe place, for comfort, for structure, for identity, for love, will not diminish; it will only grow larger. The family is the natural place to meet these needs. Acknowledge the current condition of your family, and resolve to strengthen it. Every family can be strengthened.

There is usually a "past" to resolve.
Your family is far more than you, your spouse, and your children. Your family is your family because of the influence that has been passed down for generations, whether you see or feel this or not. The

wins and successes of your parents, as well as their failures, impact you and your children greatly. Beliefs, assumptions, experiences, morals, values, and lifestyles are passed down consciously and unconsciously from one generation to the next. You can change this if you choose, but it may take several generations to fully restore and be free of what came before. The past may be something generations before, or something as recent as yesterday or this morning. Work to resolve your personal and controllable past in the present. Don't neglect it and allow it to become something that will affect your future generations.

Benefits of Strengthening Your Family

- When you strengthen your family, you strengthen yourself.
- Your family becomes a unit capable of sustaining permanent growth, for you and all members.
- You create an environment where everyone is supported, with a safety and comfort zone.
- You show your family that you value them.
- Your family environment becomes a peaceful, comfortable and sustaining place.

10 Steps to Strengthening Your Family

1. Understand that families are people, are not perfect, and can learn how to be better.
2. Understand that families are not there merely to give you everything you need; they need love and support from you as well.
3. Evaluate your current family situation and honestly determine where you can work to improve it.
4. Accept responsibility for any problems between you and other family members. Work to resolve them.
5. Adjust your attitude to work from choice, rather than obligation, within your family.
6. Accept nothing negative or unresolved with any of your children.
7. Accept nothing negative or unresolved with your current or ex-spouse/mate.
8. Accept nothing negative or unresolved with a parent.
9. Accept nothing negative or unresolved with a sibling.
10. Accept nothing negative or unresolved with any relative.

Area A: Family Communication

Perhaps the single most referenced source of a family weakening and breaking down is the lack of or poor quality of communication. Without healthy communication, families will wither and relationships will fall apart. This exercise is about increasing the amount of, the quality of, and the value of communication within your family. Honestly answer the following questions, and then develop a plan to actively build your family's communication system.

1. How would you evaluate the current state of your family's communication? Take a few minutes to jot down your thoughts about this. Is communication good, so-so, terrible, nonexistent? Why or why not?

a. With my whole immediate family (husband, wife, children, etc.)

_____

_____

_____

b. With my spouse/mate/partner

_____

_____

_____

c. With my children

_____

_____

_____

d. With my parents

_____

_____

_____

e. With my siblings

_____

_____

_____

f. With other family members

_____

_____

_____

g. With extended family (close family friends, etc.)

_____

_____

_____

_____

2. Depending upon your answers to question number one, how can you personally work to improve (all communication can be improved, no matter how good it is right now) each level of communication? Remember, this response involves you only. Decide what you can do, not what you expect others to do in each of the foregoing cases. Develop a simple action plan for each one.

a. With my whole immediate family (husband, wife, children, etc.)

_____

_____

_____

_____

b. With my spouse/mate/partner

_____

_____

_____

_____

c. With my children

_____

_____

_____

d. With my parents

_____

_____

_____

e. With my siblings

_____

_____

_____

f. With other family members

_____

_____

_____

g. With extended family (close family friends, etc.)

_____

_____

_____

Here's another question: How can you now work with others to improve their communication with you?

Credit   **A** B C

When you have honestly determined the current condition of your family's communication and have established an action plan that has been in effect for at least 30 days, give yourself credit by filling in **Area A** of this lesson on the Personal Foundation Chart.

Area B: Family Time

Another key problem area for families today is the lack of consistent and quality time together. Meals are rarely eaten together, and with both parents working, children may rarely even see their parents on weekdays. We have all read the horrifying statistics about how little time parents spend talking to their children on a daily basis. Is this the "nature of the beast," as some insist for families today, or can it be changed? Without consistent quality time, a family disintegrates. Families grow up without really knowing one another. No comfort, safety, identity, or values are shared. Families live together, but as total strangers. This exercise is designed to allow you to evaluate your actual time commitment and determine how you can improve that. Indicate how much time, on average, and the quality of that time, you spend with each of the following people in your family, and then in the space provided, show at least two things you can do differently to improve this commitment.

Real Family Time Table				
Family member (name)	**Actual time on a daily basis**	**Quality of time spent**	**What I would like for this person**	**What I can and will do to improve this (at least two action steps)**
Spouse				
Parent				
Parent				
Child				
Child				
Child				
Child				
Sibling				
Sibling				
Sibling				
Other				
Other				

Credit A **B** C
○ ● ○

When you have completed this table (answered all questions for all family members) and have successfully implemented at least one of your two stated action steps for every individual mentioned, give yourself credit by filling in **Area B** of this lesson on the Personal Foundation Chart.

Area C: Family Distractions and Detractions

Besides the key areas of communication and time, most families can list many other distractions or detractions that keep the family from being as strong and healthy as it could be. These can be anything that prevents a strong and healthy family environment. Some ideas may include things like poor nutrition or sleep habits, bad attitudes, conflicting schedules, tolerations, limited resources, etc. List the top five things that have become distractions or detractions in your family:

1. _____

2. _____

3. _____

4. _____

5. _____

Now choose the one distraction or detraction that you have the ability and power to eliminate in your family and will commit to doing so in the next 30 days.

Distraction or detraction that I will eliminate:

_____

Credit A B **C**
○ ○ ●

When you have identified the top five distractions or detractions in your family and have successfully eliminated the one you have selected, give yourself credit by filling in **Area C** of this lesson on the Personal Foundation Chart

Congratulations! You have begun a process that can continue throughout your lifetime and even affect future generations. Enjoy the new strength of your family and its support for you.

Deepen Your Community

Key Points

- You spend most of your time with your community.
- They may shape you more than you shape yourself.
- Your community includes colleagues, friends, associates, coworkers, church, and/or special interest groups.
- You attract who you are ready for.
- Your life is a response to your community.

Introduction

The notion of having and developing one's own personal community (as opposed to geographic, socioeconomic, or political communities) is becoming more common. Basically, people with similar interests and relating or communicating styles get together and stay together and eventually bond together, becoming almost as close as—and some times even closer than—a traditional family. In fact, with the introduction and accessibility of the Internet, people with very, very specific interests meet and form friendships and community that can last a lifetime.

Guiding Principle 4	**People Grow from Connection.** Connection is the wellspring of creativity.

Ask Yourself:

- Who is in my community of choice?
- Who may be part of my community whom I have not seen as such before?
- Am I currently attractive to the type of community I wish to be in?
- Do I even want to be a part of a special, chosen community?

Coaching Tips

○ It may take a while to discover, attract, or create your community of choice. As you get to know yourself better and become engaged in your life work or interests, you will draw closer to this community. Count on this concept to work, and focus on enjoying and mastering what you already have.

○ You will upgrade your community of choice several times, so the community you initially choose may end up just being a way station on your path. This is fine. But eventually, as you complete your personal and professional development, you will attract the communities that will likely be yours for a lifetime. You will be home.

Understanding Community

Communities work best when they are chosen.

The whole point of this type of community is that people come together because they want to, not because they have to. This means that you get to choose exactly who you want to be with, and you can base this choice on any number of factors—ones that mean something to you.

In order to truly choose a community, you are better off having your needs met elsewhere or being essentially needless, as described in another lesson. Only then does the group become a community of choice. If you go into a community to get needs (as opposed to wants) met, the purpose of the community is diverted. In addition, you become much less attractive to this community.

Communities bring out your best.

The real purpose or benefit of a chosen community is that you become someone even more special because you are a part of the community. The best of them brings out the best of you, and vice versa. Communities are also great for creation and creativity—the input and energy from the group, especially from such an aligned group, synthesizes with ideas readily and translates into products beneficial to all. The community you select will cause results in your life that you simply could not do on your own.

Ideally, we all elect to become part of a community because of who we will be and become, not just what we will get out of it.

Family is different from community.

Families are rearing/societal-based:

- For continuing the species (children)
- For protection of parents (care during old age)
- For approval (societal pressure)
- For love (a chance for parents and children to experience true love)

Communities are highest quality of life or choice-based:

- For enjoyment (like minds)
- For higher-end development (intellectual)
- For love, acceptance, and contribution (spiritual)

We need both. Focusing on community building puts the family structure in perspective. *(Note: you may experience community with your family. We've drawn the distinction here for those people who don't or never will. They need to develop a community that is stronger and more rewarding than what was/is based on their given family.)*

Benefits of Having a Chosen Community

- Makes you more well-rounded and well-connected; can be a reserve in case of trouble
- Expands your personal and professional horizons
- Moves you in new, more rewarding directions

10 Steps to Deepening Your Community

1. Determine who and what comprises your existing community or communities.
2. Draw a picture of your communities and show how they interrelate.
3. Examine the benefits you gain from being part of these communities, as well as potential drawbacks or roadblocks to your future development.
4. After you have honestly evaluated your existing community structure, do the benefits far outweigh the negatives?
5. Evaluate whether or not you should be part of these existing communities, and make choices and commitments to either strengthen some, remove yourself from some, or develop new ones altogether.
6. What do you offer to others as part of these existing or new communities?
7. What concrete steps can you take today, right now, to be exactly where you want to be within community?
8. Are there tolerations built into your existing communities? How can you eliminate them?
9. How can your ideal communities overlap, benefit from each other, and strengthen you so that your energy is not diverted and scattered between communities?
10. Understand that you will always be part of a community, or several, but that the choice is yours.

Area A: Upgrade Who You Know Now

This first step in attracting a community of choice is to upgrade who you currently associate with. Please complete the following checklist.

(Check items only if they are true now. Leave unchecked until they are.)

Checklist	Comments
I have a best friend whom I adore and who adores me.	
I have the perfect amount and type of friends.	
I have a strong professional network/coworkers I respect.	
The people I know professionally and personally respect me.	
I feel good enough about myself to be part of a community of choice.	
I am valued for who I am, not just for a role that I play for others.	

○ **I actively seek out people whose company I enjoy.**	
○ **I have let go of the three people in my life that drain me or that I am associated with out of obligation.**	
○ **I say no to potential friendships or relationships of any kind (business or otherwise) that just are not perfect for me.**	
○ **I am willing to be evoked, shaped, and touched by a community.**	

A B C

Credit ● ○ ○ ———————————————————————
When you have completed all 10 items, please give yourself credit by filling in
Area A of this lesson on the Personal Foundation Chart.

Area B: Designing Your Community

What is the focus or focal point of the community of which you wish to be a part? Why is it there? What's the *real* purpose of it? Please write down your thoughts below.

1. _____

2. _____

3. _____

4. _____

5. _____

Who gets to play in your community? Write down the types of people and the qualities they have that would make them a natural part of you (via the community). If you know them and they truly fit as a part of your community of choice, include their names.

1. _____

2. _____

3. _____

4. _____

5. _____

A **B** C

Credit ○ ◉ ○ _____
When you have completed these two lists and can easily and simply say who is in, or qualifies to be in, your community, give yourself credit by filling in **Area B** of this lesson on the Personal Foundation Chart.

Area C: Who You Will Become Because of Your Community

Write down the five qualities, skills, accomplishments, ways of being, and so on, that are natural for you while being a part of your chosen community. Be specific and keep it personal (*Who*-based as opposed to just *What*-based).

1. _____

2. _____

3. _____

4. _____

5. _____

A B **C**

Credit ○ ○ ◉ _____
When you have become part of the community or communities you have been describing and when you become or accomplish what you wrote down, give yourself credit by filling in **Area C** of this lesson on the Personal Foundation Chart.

Congratulations! Continue expanding, defining, and deepening your community.

Be Well Protected

Key Points

- You are fragile in many ways; you have a great deal to lose.
- You can obtain most of the protection you need.
- Protection includes covering physical assets and quality of life.
- Protection is a demonstration of responsibility.
- Acknowledge the need and just do it.

Guiding Principle 6 | **People Act in Their Own Best Interest.**
Discernment reveals the opportunities in every situation.

Introduction

It's difficult to have a strong foundation and to graduate to irresistible attraction if you have one eye on the future and one eye looking around protectively. The point here is that when fear of loss is reduced and even eliminated, you will naturally progress. The purpose of this lesson is to offer you safety.

Ask Yourself:

- What areas of my life are most susceptible to loss? (Tangibles and nontangibles)
- How can I protect myself from such losses?
- Do I have adequate protection?

Coaching Tips

○ Protection, as defined in this lesson, includes mostly the obvious needs for protection from loss such as adequate insurance and lifestyle choices that will prevent losses. However, for additional personal work, you might consider protection of spirit and mind as well as the physical. Explore how this protection might be obtained, what it would look like, and how it could be sustained. Much of the work already undertaken, and much to come, in the personal foundation program is intentionally designed to provide for spiritual, emotional, and mental well-being and protection. Obtaining well-being is one thing. Protecting it is another. It is wise to consider consistent ways to protect *all* of you, not just the physical aspects.

Understanding Protection

These are a few of the areas that should be considered for protection and safety.

Insurance

One buys insurance as a method to protect oneself against losing more money or assets than you can afford to. With insurance you reduce and transfer the financial risk by paying premiums to the insurance company. Types of insurance include:

- Health/medical
- Life
- Dental
- Disability
- Auto
- Home
- Liability/umbrella policy
- Business
- Legal

Also, another form of insurance is having two things:

- A reserve of savings
- Consistent profitability or ability to save

Systems

Systems refer to procedures, routines, support, and structures you set up to protect you from yourself, others, your environment, and life itself. Types of systems include:

- Home and car alarms
- Automated bill paying (CheckFree/Quicken) or a bill-paying service
- A CPA to do your taxes
- Family for support
- A referral/sales engine for your business
- Going to the gym or taking exercise for your heart and body
- Establishing your boundaries to protect your heart/spirit
- Living in a safe neighborhood
- Having a therapist available when needed
- Having a coach to help keep you focused
- Having your car, home, equipment inspected regularly
- Flossing (a safety system for your teeth)

Lifestyle

Lifestyle refers to the notion of selecting the type of life you want that will protect you from what you do not wish to experience or deal with in life. Designing such a lifestyle is not a form of denial or avoidance; it simply makes sense. Items include:

- Your home size/style and geographic location
- The clubs to join
- The community to enjoy
- The career/life work you select
- What you read
- Watching TV, or not
- Reading the newspaper, or not
- Where you travel
- How you spend your free time
- With whom you spend your free time
- Who your colleagues are

Benefits of Being Well Protected

- Prevention of losses
- Freedom from the stress of thinking about potential losses
- Freedom to be more focused on developing gains rather than recovering from losses
- Freedom from worry about what might happen

10 Steps to Being Well Protected

1. Determine what you have to lose.
2. Research every possible way it could be lost, and then how it can be protected.
3. Include every facet of your life, including the physical, spiritual, and emotional.
4. Do you have the resources now to handle the needed protection?
5. If not, what are you willing to accept as loss, should it happen, and what are you not willing or prepared to lose? Prioritize your loss protection list.
6. Make plans now to be well protected, in order of your established priorities.
7. Outline the steps of your plan to be well protected, and then do the first one on the list, and the next, until all are accomplished.
8. Make plans for periodic review of your list to determine how up-to-date your protection is at any given moment.
9. Be alert always to the possibility of potential losses, and how you can continually afford protection from those losses, of any kind.
10. Determine how you would recover from losses, should they happen in spite of prevention.

Area A: Insurance

Honestly evaluate your insurance needs and current insurance protection. This exercise speaks to the obvious physical insurance available to cover such things as health emergencies, loss of assets, liability, and so on. However, you might also want to consider the kind of "insurance" that is of a spiritual nature, such as friends who love and support you, a strong family, healthy communities, faith, and other things that will help you deal with losses that are not physical, and will insure that you will not lose those spiritual things most important to you. Consider spending time journaling about this vital area.

Consider the following statements. Use a worksheet to write down all the ways you need to be and can be protected from loss. Follow the 10 steps just provided. Once you have done this, determine if the following statements are true for you. Check each off if they are. If not, do what is necessary to make them true for you.

- I have plenty of insurance.
- I have a minimum of $10,000 in savings that I do not need in the next 12 months.
- I save consistently and wouldn't think of not saving.

A B C

Credit ● ○ ○

When all statements are true, give yourself credit by filling in **Area A** of this lesson on the Personal Foundation Chart.

Area B: Safety Systems

Safety systems are sets of procedures or other things that when practiced or used together form a sort of safety net to protect you from loss. These systems may be as simple as a set of personal guidelines or rules you follow, boundaries, people, or other combinations of things that you rely upon to keep you safe. Safety may involve preventing the loss of physical assets as well as the loss of such things as clients, reputation, spiritual well-being, and the like. Consider every area of your life as you complete the following.

List 10 systems that keep you safe. If you cannot list 10, think of some that perhaps you need to initiate or have in place.

1. _____

2. _____

3. _____

4. _____

5. _____

6. _____

7. _____

8. _____

9. _____

10. _____

A **B** C

Credit ◯●◯   When you have 10 systems in place, give yourself credit by filling in **Area B** of this lesson on the Personal Foundation Chart.

Area C: Lifestyle

Consider the life you want to lead in order to be well protected and safe. How does that lifestyle look? Create 10 statements about that well-protected life and your attitude and behavior in it.

1. _____

2. _____

3. _____

4. _____

5. _____

6. _____

7. _____

8. _____

9. _____

10. _____

Now comes the hard part. What steps are needed in order for your life to look just like the 10 statements you have created? Make plans to do what is necessary to implement and live them.

	Currently true? If not, how can it be, and when?
1.	
2.	
3.	
4.	
5.	
6.	
7.	
8.	
9.	
10.	

A B **C**

Credit ○ ○ ●

When you have implemented or upgraded the 10 key aspects of your lifestyle, give yourself credit by filling in **Area C** of this lesson on the Personal Foundation Chart

Congratulations! Enjoy being well protected and the peace of mind it allows.

Become a Problem-Free Zone

Key Points

- It is normal to experience problems in life.
- Problems afford us opportunities to win.
- A strong personal foundation minimizes problems.
- People do not have to be problems.
- Becoming a problem-free zone frees up valuable time.
- When problems occur, they are quickly resolved.

Introduction

It's pretty safe to say that most of us have problems. We can probably also state that we have had something to do with those problems. While we can acknowledge personal responsibility for problems and the need to handle, solve, and even eliminate them, we should also say that we could avoid most of them.

This lesson presents the opportunity to look at problems differently. Yes, they are yours to handle, but it helps to understand where problems come from, what fixes them permanently, and what prevents problems so you can enjoy the comfort and lifestyle of being a problem-free zone.

Guiding Principle 7 | **People Live from Their Perception.**
An inclusive, present-based perception of reality
is the platform for effective action.

Ask Yourself:

- How do I define "problems"?
- Is my life characterized by problems?
- Do I seem to experience more than my share of problems?
- Is there a consistent pattern to my problems?
- Am I ready to be a problem-free zone, or do I enjoy, somehow gain comfort or pleasure from, my problems?

Coaching Tips

○ Different people define problems in different ways. Some people see them as challenges, some as great obstacles, some as depressing burdens, some as nuisances. The dictionary defines a problem as anything involving doubt, uncertainty, or difficulty. It generally implies that some condition exists that requires a solution or an answer. Problems often arise from not learning previous lessons or gaining insights from previous messages. We should avoid the tendency to place blame for a problem, whether on ourselves or on others. The focus should be on resolving the problem and ending up with a positive instead of a negative. The first step toward being a problem-free zone is to identify existing problems and solve them. The next step is to determine how to avoid problems. Problems are not resolved by avoidance, denial, or blame, but by serious and honest evaluation of your personal foundation, which tends to attract or repel problems. Being a problem-free zone requires honest, straightforward searching for answers and diligent maintenance of your established personal foundation. This lesson is intended to advance and widen that foundation, allowing you to focus your energies on growth, not continual problem solving.

Understanding a Problem-Free Zone

Integrity + Boundaries + Standards = Problem-Free Zone

Have you ever noticed how some people simply do not have problems, or at least fewer than most? And others attract enough problems to continuously keep their plate full? Why is that? Living in integrity, where every area of your life is part of a healthy whole, and resisting the potential for "disintegration" by insisting on living the standards you have set and maintaining your personal and professional boundaries will create a "problem avoidance system" for you. Living in integrity, setting boundaries, abiding by standards, and working with your family and friends to understand and respect them is an investment that heads off many, if not most, of life's problems.

Encourage those around you to also be problem-free zones.

You may be the first one on your block to adopt a problem-free lifestyle, so it will be up to you to teach others in your family and community about this notion. You will find that about half the folks will want to become a problem-free zone and half actually enjoy their problems—even need their problems. The latter will have a very, very difficult time outgrowing their problems. You will need to decide what to do about this.

Benefits of Becoming a Problem-Free Zone

- Life becomes happier, easier, less stressful.
- You are in control, not the problems.
- You live a consistent, strong personal foundation that repels problems.
- Your energy is not constantly drained away by preventable problems.
- Your attitude is better, more positive, more caring.

10 Steps to Becoming a Problem-Free Zone

1. Evaluate your existing problems honestly. Try to determine a common source or common reason for them.
2. Is that common source something you have control over? If so, what can you do about it?
3. Determine if you are willing to resolve current problems and avoid new ones.
4. Be aware of and sensitive to conditions that have created problems in the past.
5. Understand that you have the choice to attract or repel problems, and all that this means for you.

6. Plan to eliminate all current problems in a way that will prevent them from recurring in the future. There is always a solution to every problem if you are willing.
7. Examine your attitude about problems. Do you enjoy them? Be honest. Do they stimulate or challenge you, or drain you? Are you willing to change this attitude?
8. Evaluate the problems you apparently have no control over. Is this really true? Being very creative, what actually could you do to prevent experiencing even these as problems?
9. If you are ready to become a problem-free zone, it requires a firm commitment on your part. Make it and abide by it.
10. Develop a "problem awareness" early warning system. How can you spot potential problems and head them off before they actually become a problem for you?

Area A: Solve Your Current Problems

Yes, you *can* do it. There is always a solution for every problem. It just depends on how willing you are to accept it and act on it. Make a list of 10 problems you have at this moment. Use the table to create possible (that's *possible*) solutions. If you can't see a solution, use a coach, a good trusted friend, another set of eyes to help you see things you might be missing. Make sure the solutions are indeed possible. Then, make a commitment to resolve them *all* in the next 30 days, or as quickly as you can. Check them off when they are permanently resolved.

	Current Problem	Possible Solution	Resolved
1.			
2.			
3.			
4.			
5.			
6.			
7.			
8.			
9.			
10.			

A B C

Credit ●○○

When you have identified your top 10 problems and solved them, give yourself credit by filling in **Area A** of this lesson on the Personal Foundation Chart.

Area B: Prevent Future Problems

Being a problem-free zone means that not only do you not allow current problems to exist in your life, but you also do what is necessary to prevent future problems. What do you need to do that will head off problems in the future? Please write down five things you can do now.

1. _____

2. _____

3. _____

4. _____

5. _____

Personal Foundation Idea Bank

1. Complete the Personal Foundation program.
2. Have a coach.
3. Get your energy from a source other than problems.
4. Stop spending time with people who give you problems or who enjoy problems.
5. Have a reserve of cash, time, energy, and space so that problems will generally stay away.
6. Have better things to do during your day and lifetime than solving problems.
7. Be focused on a project or on your life in such a way that there are no openings for problems.
8. Stop tolerating anything and everything.
9. Delegate the problems you come across to a proven problem solver.
10. Stop causing problems for yourself.

A **B** C

Credit ○●○

When you have identified and put into practice five ways to prevent future problems, give yourself credit by filling in **Area B** of this lesson on the Personal Foundation Chart.

Area C: Become a Problem-Free Zone

You are already pretty close, given your work on Areas A and B. But there are still probably five more things to do that only you know about in order to make yourself a problem-free zone. Please identify and write these down on the lines provided. Then handle them. Ask friends, family, and a coach for help.

1. _____

2. _____

3. _____

4. _____

5. _____

Credit

A B **C**
◯ ◯ ⬤

When you have done these five things and have been problem free for 60 days, give yourself credit by filling in **Area C** of this lesson on the Personal Foundation Chart.

Congratulations! You will find that you will not want to live anywhere but in the problem-free zone ever again.

Guiding Principle 8 | **People Have a Choice.**
Awareness is the precursor to choice.

NeedLess Program

It is possible to have all of your needs met permanently. Now, that might make your life just a bit too effortless, but we hear that people find some rewarding way to fill up the time that is freed up when not chasing needs.

This three step program is designed to be used in conjunction with a professional coach. But you can start the process by completing the steps outlined here.

It takes most people about a year to reach the 25-point level for all four needs. Have it be a great time in your life. You needn't suffer as you get your needs fully satisfied.

Purpose of the Program

The purpose of the **NeedLess** program process is to help you to:

- Identify what your Personal Needs are
- Understand how to get your Personal Needs met
- Design an effective system to have them vanish

What Are Personal Needs?

Personal needs (versus body needs such as water, food, shelter, and love) are those things we must have in order to be our best. One can get through life fairly well not having these needs met, but for an effortless, rewarding, and successful life, personal needs must be identified, addressed, and handled.

Many of us spend our lives trying (consciously or not) to get these needs met. At best, we treat the symptoms or get temporary relief from them. This is for two reasons: most of us assume these needs will "always be with us" and that's "just the way we are." This is not true.

It does take a special technique to handle personal needs once and for all. We call that the NeedLess process. Your professional coach can assist you to more fully understand the dynamic of needs and the steps to have them vanish.

Progress Chart

Date	Points (+/-)	Score

NeedLess Program 100-Point Checklist

#	Top Four Needs			
	1	**2**	**3**	**4**
25				
24				
23				
22				
21				
20				
19				
18				
17				
16				
15				
14				
13				
12				
11				
10				
9				
8				
7				
6				
5				
4				
3				
2				
1				

Give yourself credit as you get points from the 100-point program. Fill in columns from the bottom up.

Instructions

Please read these instructions twice, and read them carefully to let the subtleties show themselves.

Step 1: Select 10 Needs

Read the list of needs and circle approximately 10 that resonate as a need for you. You are looking for a need—not a want, a should, a fantasy, or a wish. A need is something that must be met for you to be your best. Part of the first step is to tell the truth about what you actually need. This may be the first time you have ever admitted this to yourself. Some of these you will know innately. Others require some straight looking. Please be willing to "try on" words you might normally skip over. These may be hidden needs. If so, you may have one or more of the following reactions:

- "No, no, no; I don't want that to be a need."
- You can't get to the next word quickly enough.
- "If that were true, I'd have to change my life a lot!"
- Flush, blush, or shake when reading the word.

Now circle the 10 words you believe to be personal needs. Ask yourself: "If I had this, would I be able to reach my goals and vision without effort?" (work yes, struggle no).

Step 2: Narrow Your Needs to 4

We all need a little of everything listed on this page. But we want you to pick the four personal needs from the ones you circled. You may wish to compare each of your 10 needs with each other and ask yourself "Now, do I need X or Y? Which ones could I live well without? Which ones, when met, make the other ones not as important?" Choose your four personal needs and write them down on the top of the checklist provided.

Be Accepted	Approved Be popular Tolerated	Be included Sanctioned	Respected Cool	Permitted Allowed
To Accomplish	Achieve Profit Victory	Fulfill Attain	Realize Yield	Reach Consummate
Be Acknowledged	Be worthy Complimented Thanked	Be praised Be prized	Honored Appreciated	Flattered Valued
Be Loved	Liked Be desired Be touched	Cherished Be preferred	Esteemed Be relished	Held fondly Be adored
Be Right	Correct Be deferred to Understood	Not mistaken Be confirmed	Honest Be advocated	Morally right Be encouraged
Be Cared For	Get attention Be attended to Embraced	Be helped Be treasured	Cared about Tenderness	Be saved Get gifts

Certainty	Clarity Guarantees Precision	Accuracy Promises	Assurance Commitments	Obviousness Exactness
Be Comfortable	Luxury Indulgence Served	Opulence Abundance	Excess Not work	Prosperity Taken care of
To Communicate	Be heard Share Informed	Gossip Talk	Tell stories Be listened to	Make a point Comment
To Control	Dictate to Correct others Restrict	Command Be obeyed	Restrain Not ignored	Manage Keep status quo
Be Needed	Improve others Affect others Be a critical link	Be useful Need to give	Be craved Be important	Please others Be material
Duty	Obligated Satisfy others Do the right thing	Follow Prove self	Obey Be devoted	Have a task Have a cause
Be Free	Unrestricted Autonomous Liberated	Privileged Sovereign	Immune Not obligated	Independent Self-reliant
Honesty	Forthrightness Loyalty Tell all	Uprightness Frankness	No lying No censoring	Sincerity No secrets
Order	Perfection Checklists Regulated	Symmetry Unvarying	Consistent Proper	Sequential Literalness
Peace	Quietness Stillness Steadiness	Calmness Balance	Unity Agreements	Reconciliation Respite
Power	Authority Strength Influence	Capacity Might	Results Stamina	Omnipotence Prerogative
Recognition	Be noticed Get credit Celebrated	Be remembered Acclaim	Be known for Heeded	Regarded well Seen
Safety	Security Deliberate	Protected Vigilant	Stable Cautious Alert	Fully informed Guarded
Work	Career Make it happen Be busy	Performance At task	Vocation Responsibility	Press, push Industriousness

Step 3: Create a System to Get Your Needs Met

Now that you have your personal needs identified, you will want to design a way to have them all met, permanently. This satisfaction system has three parts, as described below:

Establishing Boundaries

A boundary is a line you draw all around you that permits only the behaviors of others that are acceptable and nourishing to you. You may set a boundary of not allowing anyone to hit you, yell at you, be critical of you, take advantage of you, not show affection, call you only when they need something, interrupt you when you are working, etc. You may be permitting these behaviors now for some pretty good reasons. But there are no excuses or reasons to let anyone do anything to you that hurts you, distracts you, uses you or commands your attention. You will want to establish a boundary that is much more than you actually need. Be rigorous with yourself on this one. You cannot get your needs met if you are unwilling to set significant boundaries, so no excuses. Be selfish on this one!

When you set a boundary, you are protecting your heart, soul and what we call self. So, you cannot be your self without the protection provided by strong, healthy boundaries. The people who really care about you will honor these boundaries, and will care for you more, but give everyone time to get used to them.

Getting A Selfish Automatic Sprinkler System

Once boundaries are identified and installed, the next step is to design what we call a Selfish Automatic Sprinkler System, or SASS. A SASS is just what the term implies. You want your need to be satisfied (watered) whether you're thinking about it or not (automatic). This takes a little creative work to put together—your professional coach has experience with this one and is a good person with whom to brainstorm.

SASS examples include: getting friends to satisfy your need by saying or doing specific things you have designed for them to do, like calling you, including you, doing things for you (that you asked for), telling you how they appreciate you, etc. You will want to be shameless in this process of designing and implementing a SASS. It is good to tell the people around you how they can satisfy your needs. Remember, it is only temporary, because when done properly, these needs vanish.

Raising Your Personal Standards

After you have started on boundaries and your SASS, begin to substantially raise your personal standards. PS's are the behaviors you hold your self to—to become a bigger person. Examples of PS's range from the obvious to the advanced: don't steal, always tell the truth, speak straight, be unconditionally constructive, be responsible for how you are heard not what you say, don't smoke or abuse your body, always be early, avoid all adrenaline rushes.

Set PS's which are a stretch, but not ones which will cause you to fail. You will have plenty of time to upgrade them with the extra energy you receive as your needs become met.

NeedLess Program Checklist

Use this checklist to guide yourself through the program. Fill in the circle when you have *started* on the step. Fill in the square when you have *completed* the step. Fill in the appropriate box on the checklist provided when you have completed the step. Work these 25 steps in order.

Do this process for each of the four needs you've chosen as personal needs.

1. Select the personal needs, using the procedure described in step one. Write in the needs at the top of the checklist provided.

2. Ask yourself "Why is this need important enough to me to be a Personal Need?" Write down five specific reasons on a sheet of paper.

3. Ask "Who am I when I get this need met? How do I act? What do I think about? What motivates me?" Write down five specific examples on a piece of paper.

4. Ask "Who am I not when I don't get this need met? How do I behave? How do I feel about myself? About others? About life?" Write down five specific responses on a piece of paper.

5. Ask "How well am I getting this need met? What am I doing in my life that permits this need to be satisfied to the point of it vanishing?" Write down five specific ways that you are currently satisfying this need.

6. Ask "Where am I not getting this need met? What am I doing that restricts, dishonors or does not give this need the room and nourishment it requires and deserves?" Write down five specific things you are doing which don't serve your needs.

7. Ask "What three changes would I make in my life in order to fully meet and satisfy this need?" Write down the three specific (and probably large) changes to make in the next 90 days. Examples of changes: change jobs, face and handle something tough, stop smoking, start fully communicating, let go of duties, get special training, let go of the future, let go of draining people.

8. Make change #1—permanently.

9. Make change #2—permanently.

10. Make change #3—permanently.

11. Ask "What are the three boundaries I can install to protect myself so that this need has a chance of getting met? What do I no longer permit others (or situations) to do to or with me?" List these on paper.

12. Install each of these three boundaries to a degree greater than you need.

○ □ 13. Ask "What are the three things that people must do for me to satisfy this need?" (SASS). Write these down on a piece of paper.

○ □ 14. Arrange for SASS 1.

○ □ 15. Arrange for SASS 2.

○ □ 16. Arrange for SASS 3.

○ □ 17. Ask "What are the three high personal standards which I must honor in order for this need to vanish?" List these on paper.

○ □ 18. Honor high personal standard #1.

○ □ 19. Honor high personal standard #2.

○ □ 20. Honor high personal standard #3.

○ □ 21. Ask "What must I now upgrade in my life to have this need fully satisfied forever?" Come up with three substantial changes.

○ □ 22. Make these changes.

○ □ 23. Eliminate any residue or clean up anything left from this process.

○ □ 24. Share this process with a friend and help them get started with it.

○ □ 25. Throw a party to celebrate your new life.

Intellectual Property Notice

Resources

Attention Readers:

Thank you for participating in the collective wisdom of Coach U. Together, we all continue to learn. Additional resources and forms can be found in the *Coach U's Essential Coaching Tools: Your Complete Practice Resource* book by Coach U, Inc.

Attention CoachInc.com Students and Graduates:

CoachInc.com students and graduates may find additional and/or more recent resources associated with this module in the resource area of the student-only website. If you are a student or graduate of one of CoachInc.com's ICF-accredited coach training programs, you can access these by searching under the name of the course. When the course description page appears you may find a link to the list of additional resources. Each item is a live link to its actual location on the website. Click on the item to access the information.

Do remember to take the associated online self-test for this module once you have completed the course in-person or by TeleClass. The tests are required for coach certification with the International Coach Federation. Throughout the course or anytime you find valuable resources for a particular course please feel free to add to the value of our curriculum by forwarding the resource to revampteam@coachu.com.

www.coachinc.com

Personal Foundation
Level 3

Overview

○ **Benefits** Go to Page > 133

By fully participating in the material offered in this module, you will be significantly strengthening and improving your personal foundation through work on the *How* component.

○ **Definitions** Go to Page > 134

Please refer to the Definitions section of the Introduction to Personal Foundation module.

○ **Concepts** Go to Page > 135

What Is Personal Foundation?: The *How* Component

Your personal foundation is your structural basis that supports you in living an exceptional life. We have called this third part the *How* of personal foundation, as it defines and discusses how a person sustains their authentic self.

○ **Distinctions** Go to Page > 137

No Distinctions are provided with this module.

○ **Application** Go to Page > 138

The Application section of each personal foundation module contain the lessons that are the personal application and learning for developing a strong foundation. This module contains seven lessons relating to the *How* component of personal foundation.

Reorient Around Your Values: Your values are ideals that are personally important and meaningful for you and draw you forward. This lesson asks you to set up your life so that you are making choices and taking actions that fully express your core values.

Invest in Your Life: You are a great investment, assuming you are ready to benefit from that which you choose to invest.

Choose Your Work to Be You: This is a design-it-yourself lesson. Only you can ask the right questions, make the right choices, and take the right actions regarding your life work.

Choose a Healthy Attitude: A healthy attitude allows us to respond evenly, positively, and in balance and control at all times. The purpose of this lesson is to assist you in choosing the attitude that preserves your sense of well-being.

Create a Reserve: To have a reserve means that you have more than you need, often so much more that you essentially have no needs.

Start Attracting: As we develop, we prefer to become attractive to opportunities, ourselves, others, potential customers, and the future, rather than becoming better at promoting, marketing, seducing, controlling, or manipulating.

Perfect the Present: The ways things are today are that way for a good reason (even if you can't see or understand the reason). It is a lesson just to understand that the present is perfect.

Benefits

By fully participating in the material offered in this module, you will be significantly strengthening and improving your personal foundation through work on the *How* component. You will learn how to be the real you.

This module is designed to allow you to:

O **Work** through seven lessons that will dramatically affect the *How* of your personal foundation

O **Discover** how you can integrate your values into every area of your life, make smart and fruitful investments in yourself, carefully consider your work to be you, choose a healthy attitude, simplify your life, and create reserves

O **Understand** the set of processes, methods, and values that drives your behavior

O **Know** exactly *How* you act in order to be your authentic self

O **Begin** to segue from Coach U's Personal Foundation program to Coach U's Irresistible Attraction program

Definitions

Please refer to the Definitions section of the Introduction to Personal Foundation module.

Concepts

What Is Personal Foundation?: The *How* Component

Your personal foundation is your structural basis that supports you in living an exceptional life. Just as a house must be built on a strong foundation to avoid collapsing under stress, so must your life. A house's foundation is made up of earth, cement, and steel. Your personal foundation is also made up of three major elements.

Humans are complex creatures. Volumes have been written about the various components, physical and otherwise, that comprise an individual. Essentially, however, all that we are can be summed up in three parts we often call body, mind, and spirit. To simplify the understanding of these parts, and ultimately the refining and growth of the whole, this personal foundation program will label them the *What*, *Who*, and *How* of every person.

This module contains lessons relating to the How *of personal foundation.*

The *How*

The third component of personal foundation is the set of processes, methods, and values that drives our behavior—*How* we do the things we do, and *How* we are *Who* we are. The fuel for the *How* of us is the *Who*, which essentially yields the *What*. If you put this into an equation it would look like this:

Who + How = What

The *What* equates to part of the three major elements—the body, mind and spirit. The mind drives our actions based upon the essence of the spirit. The *What* of us is, essentially, "where the rubber meets the road," where the behaviors are spawned and where the action is planned and executed. The result of this process gives us the *What*—the presenting part of us seen by the world.

Relating back to the Five-S Model, the *shifts* and *solutions* sides of the model are integrated with the *What* of us. The practical and application sides of learning and growth happen in the *How*. The learning begins in the *Who* but translates into application in the *How*. The actual work of personal development most likely happens here, and most directly affects the growth of an individual. This is where new behaviors and skills are practiced, cementing the new behaviors. The *How* is also in need of continual upkeep and maintenance, just like any finely tuned engine. Adjustments, regular "servicing," and "tune-ups" keep the *How* functioning smoothly and the engine traveling forward.

The Application section of this module contains the lessons pertaining to the *How* of personal foundation and includes:

- Reorient Around Your Values
- Invest in Your Life
- Choose Your Work to Be You
- Choose a Healthy Attitude
- Create a Reserve
- Start Attracting
- Perfect Your Present

" The most important part of **do**ctrine is the first two letters. **"** | **David C. Egner**

Distinctions

Because of the somewhat different nature of the contents of the personal foundation modules, no "Distinctions" are provided here. The lessons contained in the "Application" section of each of the four personal foundation modules are relatively self-contained and self-explanatory.

Application

This section is composed of seven different lessons:

- Reorient Around Your Values
- Invest in Your Life
- Choose Your Work to Be You
- Choose a Healthy Attitude
- Create a Reserve
- Start Attracting
- Perfect Your Present

Work your way through all seven lessons and be sure to color in the appropriate "Credit" boxes on your Personal Foundation Chart.

Reorient Around Your Values

Key Points

- Your values are worth discovering.
- Values are the only sustainable basis for goal setting.
- Personal foundation *affords* a values reorientation.
- You are your values.
- Values bring fulfillment; wants bring gratification.

Introduction

You have many options for orienting your life around, including needs, wants, the future, and key values. Your values are ideals that are personally important and meaningful for you and draw you forward. This lesson asks you to set up your life so that you are making choices and taking actions that fully express your core values.

Ask Yourself:
- What are my values?
- What are *your* values?
- Is it possible to reorient my entire life around values?
- What would that look like?
- Would this be considered selfish?

" Values are like fingerprints. Nobody's are the same, but you leave 'em all over everything you do. " | **Elvis Presley**

Coaching Tips

○ Work toward discovering your life purpose as expressed by your number one value.

Understanding Values

You are your values.
Values are that part of you which is you. Values are what you are naturally inclined to do, are drawn toward or are eager to do, without effort or even goal setting. For example, some people are natural explorers—they were adventuresome at age six and at age 40 they are still taking adventure trips. Pretty obviously exploring is a value for them. A person with that value doesn't have to make themselves go explore—they just do. Values determine who you are, what you want, and how you live.

Values are easily squashed by needs, "shoulds," and problems.
While values run deep within us, they tend to get covered over or become transparent when other, more powerful distractions command our attention. These distractions come in many forms, but many of the most powerful are:

- Needs
- Shoulds
- Tolerations
- Unresolved matters
- Adrenaline
- Addictions
- Irresponsibility
- Stress
- Fantasies
- Roles
- Money
- Obligation/duty

Through coaching and completion of this program, however, the distracting power of these things lessens and your values become more apparent. Eventually, almost naturally, you can orient your life around these values. Until the previous list is handled, however, the values orientation is difficult to do, because most people have values and needs confused—their needs are so great that they overshadow their values. This circumstance makes living a values-based life and setting values-based goals unsustainable.

Guiding Principle 9 | **People Define Their Own Integrity.**
The vigilant development of the fit between calling and conduct creates integrity.

Values-based goals bring fulfillment.

If getting what you want makes you happy, and if getting your needs met brings satisfaction, then living a values-based life brings fulfillment. Fulfillment is that inner feeling beyond happiness or satisfaction—it's that lasting glow and the feeling of being totally you.

Benefits of Orienting Around Values

- Goal setting is easier and goals can be reached more quickly.
- Your life purpose or vision comes to you more clearly.
- Fewer distractions occur; life is simple but rich.

10 Steps to Reorienting Around Values

1. Understand that everything you do, feel, and think is shaped by your values.
2. Spend time identifying, expanding, defining, and tailoring your values.
3. Eliminate all "shoulds" from your values. ("Shoulds" are choices that we make based on the opinions and needs of others, rather than our own.)
4. Do you "like" your chosen values? (This is the same as asking if you like who you are. We can change values, but it is not easy and involves intense personal work and raw honesty.) If not, why not, and what can you do about it?
5. Write your personal mission or vision in life.
6. Does this mission match your values? If not, make appropriate adjustments.
7. Consider what you "do" in life—your career, your relationships, everything. Do these things match your identified values? If not, why not? How can you bring them into alignment?
8. Spend time with others who share your values.
9. Look for opportunities that reinforce your values.
10. Set up an automatic mental system whereby you always measure your actions against your values.

Area A: Identify Five Key Values

Key values are those interests and qualities that have always intrigued you or to which you have always been attracted.

Step 1.
Select 20 values that naturally appeal to you (not needs, shoulds, role-based duties, etc.).

Adventure	Beauty	To Catalyze	To Contribute
○ Risk	○ Grace	○ Impact	○ Serve
○ The unknown	○ Refinement	○ Move forward	○ Improve
○ Thrill	○ Elegance	○ Touch	○ Augment
○ Danger	○ Attractiveness	○ Turn on	○ Assist
○ Speculation	○ Loveliness	○ Unstick others	○ Endow
○ Dare	○ Radiance	○ Coach	○ Strengthen
○ Gamble	○ Magnificence	○ Spark	○ Facilitate
○ Endeavor	○ Gloriousness	○ Encourage	○ Minister to
○ Quest	○ Taste	○ Influence	○ Grant
○ Experiment		○ Stimulate	○ Provide
○ Exhilaration		○ Energize	○ Foster
○ Venture		○ Alter	○ Assist
		○ Repair/Fix	

To Create	To Discover	To Feel	To Lead
○ Design	○ Learn	○ Experience displaying emotions	○ Guide
○ Invent	○ Detect	○ Sense	○ Inspire
○ Synthesize	○ Perceive	○ To glow	○ Influence
○ Imagination	○ Locate	○ To feel good	○ Cause
○ Ingenuity	○ Realize	○ Be with	○ Arouse
○ Originality	○ Uncover	○ Energy flow	○ Interest
○ Conceive	○ Discern	○ In touch with sensations	○ Reign
○ Plan	○ Distinguish		○ Govern
○ Build	○ Observe		○ Rule
○ Perfect			○ Persuade
○ Assemble			○ Encourage
○ Inspire			○ Model

Mastery	Pleasure	To Relate	Be Sensitive
○ Expert	○ Have fun	○ Be connected	○ Tenderness
○ Dominate field	○ Sensual	○ Part of community	○ Touch
○ Adept	○ Physical	○ Family	○ Perceive
○ Superiority	○ Bliss	○ To unite	○ Be present
○ Primacy	○ Be amused	○ To nurture	○ Empathize
○ Preeminence	○ Be entertained	○ Be linked	○ Support
○ Greatest	○ Play games	○ Be bonded	○ Show compassion
○ Best	○ Sports	○ Be integrated	○ Respond
○ Outdo		○ Be with	○ See
○ Set standards			
○ Excellence			

Be Spiritual	To Teach	To Win	Other
Be aware	Educate	Prevail	
Be accepting	Instruct	Accomplish	
Be awake	Enlighten	Attain	
Relate with God	Inform	Score	
Devoting	Prepare	Acquire	
Holy	Edify	Win over	
Honoring	Prime	Triumph	
Be passionate	Uplift	Predominate	
Religious	Explain	Attract	

Step 2.

Now, toss out the needs and "shoulds" from your list. Evaluate your chosen values:

- If you need it to be happy, it's a need, not a value.
- If you are doing it in order to get something else, it is not a value.
- If you want it, but it doesn't come easily, it is probably a "should."
- If you did it when you were eight years old, it is probably a value.
- If it is really exciting and you're afraid of it, it may be a value.

Please add more, or prune, to bring your true value list to a total of five. List them in the space provided:

My five true values are:

1. _____

2. _____

3. _____

4. _____

5. _____

A B C

Credit ●○○

When you have completed steps one and two, give yourself credit by filling in **Area A** of this lesson on the Personal Foundation Chart.

Area B: Fully Reorient Around One of Your Key Values

1. Pick one value and take 10 steps to honor it.

From your five true values, select one to work on. Then make a list of the 10 big or little life changes to make in order for that one value to be honored. These 10 items should be attainable within 90 days. Perhaps the value won't be fully expressed or honored, but you will have a sense of what it is like to have your life revolve around this value. These 10 steps are changes to make in your life to *allow* the value to be expressed. Here is an example list:

Sample Value = Creativity

10 Sample Steps:

1. Let go of projects or commitments that don't allow you to be creative.
2. Surround yourself with three friends who are very creative and learn from them.
3. Take an art class.
4. Ask people what they see you being naturally creative at.
5. Stop tolerating the circumstances that diminish your creativity.
6. Pick a goal that you can reach by the end of the year.
7. Pick a goal that shows you are serious about this value.
8. Pick a goal that is something you would enjoy doing, not "should" do.
9. Ask your friends and your coach what goals they see for you.
10. Pick a fresh goal; no recycling allowed.

2. Select or design an exciting project to fully express one value.

Continuing with the sample "Creativity" value, design a project or goal that will reinforce that you are very creative. For example:

- Teach a class in being creative.
- Sculpt for the first time.
- Make words up.
- Redecorate.
- Design a $1,000,000 financial independence plan for yourself.

Make the project big enough to command your attention for between six months and one year. Remember, orienting your life around your values is a skill. It takes time and support to move through the space to make living this way natural.

A B C

Credit ○ ⬤ ○ ——————————————

When your life is clearly and fully oriented around this one key value, give yourself credit by filling in **Area B** of this lesson on the Personal Foundation Chart.

Area C: Reorient Around All Five Key Values

Reorganize your entire life around your other four key values. Now it is time for the big stuff. You may need to do the following kinds of things in order to accomplish the reorientation:

- Adjust your priorities.
- Change jobs/occupations.
- Moonlight, making money from what you *value*.
- Stop tolerating.
- Build a community of creative people around you.
- Move to the geographic location of your choice.

Area C takes time, time, and more time, so don't rush it. When you are ready, your values will *pull* you, rather than you *pushing* them. Give yourself that time and space.

Note: The objective here is to have only value-based goals this year. If you have a goal that does not fit with one of your top five values, either adapt the goal to fit the value or get rid of it and come up with another. Do not adapt the value to the goal. And only have one goal per value. You are using your values as the reference point in your life—not your goals. That is what makes this process so exciting.

A B C
Credit ◯◯⬤ — When your life is clearly and fully oriented around all five of your key values, give yourself credit by filling in **Area C** of this lesson on the Personal Foundation Chart.

Congratulations! **Enjoy finally living a life aligned with your values.** All of life becomes easier and more natural now.

Invest in Your Life

Key Points

- You *can* invest well in yourself, forever.
- Use a coach to identify where to invest now.
- Enjoy your investment.
- Expect a lifetime of investment return.
- Invest in others.

Introduction

You are your greatest investment, assuming you are ready to benefit from where and in what you choose to invest. There are three key areas of life worthy of conscious investment in self:

- Your advanced personal development
- Your quality of life, today
- Your ability to earn or make money

Ask Yourself:

- How do I make a conscious effort to invest in myself?
- Have I ever done this, and planned for it?
- Why is this a good idea?
- What would it take for me to make this a priority?

Coaching Tips

○ It is vital to begin this lesson by understanding that you are worthy of every investment you choose to make in yourself. Quite often we evaluate investments according to whether or not they are *worth* the investment—of time, money, or energy. While this can be helpful in determining your level of participation in other types of investments, always remember that *you are worth* any investment. The investment itself may not be worthy of your commitment, but *you are worth* it. Investments are made with the specific intention of receiving a benefit. *You* are worth that benefit. Frequently there is an underlying, and sometimes undetected, current of thought within us that somehow says we aren't worthy of investment. Don't buy into this. You are absolutely worth it. Don't allow your self-worth to be an issue in these decisions. Settle this once and for all. *You are worth it.*

Understanding Investing in Your Life

While there are definitely other areas of personal investment, these are considered key for optimal enjoyment and fulfillment in life.

Your Marketable Skills

People pay you money because you have something they want, whether it is a skill, product, service, time, or solutions. And, people are generally thrifty and value-oriented, so expect to give more than you think you should for whatever amount you are being paid. Marketable skills include the obvious like typing, management and technical skills, but they also include the following transportable skills:

- Problem solving
- Good judgment
- Ability to hear what is really being asked for or said (listening skills)
- Wisdom and discernment
- Ability to take charge and make something happen
- Ability to coach others to accomplish more
- Timing
- Organizational skills
- Awareness of trends and patterns
- Ability to forecast the future, based on what is occurring today
- Ability to find the language to express all that you think and feel
- And many more . . .

Your Ability to Attract the Right People and Opportunities

To ensure profitability, often you need only attract and keep the right people around you who find your structure, energy, and vision to be evocative, nourishing, and compelling. Here are some of the skills, attainments, and qualities to invest in the development of:

- Your personality
- The way you relate with others
- The effect you have on others
- Articulating a big and compelling enough vision to attract others
- Your personal foundation so that you attract only the best because you are your best

Your Ability to Manage and Reinvest What You Earn

This area is usually best delegated to a gifted or skilled group of people, including:

- CPA
- Money manager
- Executive team
- Managers
- Board of directors

Advanced Personal Development

You could invest hundreds of thousands of dollars in your personal development if you had the time and funds to do so. The key is to select exactly the parts of you that you want developed. Here are some areas, but there are many more. Ask your coach or other advisor for additional ideas.

- Listening
- Relating
- Attraction
- Flow
- Spirituality
- Energy

Your Quality of Life, Today

Invest in a high quality of life. By high quality of life, we don't mean Tiffany's instead of K-Mart or success instead of failure. High quality of life refers to how you are doing, feeling, being, and accomplishing each day, without having to use a measure. You are the only one who knows if your current quality of life is high or low. When you spend your time and energy focusing on tomorrow's quality of life, you will consequently miss out on today's. When you do this, today's quality is not what it should be. You can do things to improve your life quality in this moment, in this day. Make this a priority. If you focus on how good today can be, and is, and do all you can to make it the highest quality it can be for you, your future's quality is automatically raised.

Ability to Make or Earn Money

The nature of life dictates that most, if not all, of us need to earn a living. We make choices about the work we do, how much we do, and the standard of living we either need or want. Most of us desire to make more money than we do currently. To make more money, there are three areas where you may need to invest some seed money (thus, the old adage: it takes money to make money).

Benefits of Investing in Your Life

- You will have a sense of self-worth.
- You will consistently receive fulfilling returns on your investments.
- You will feel more in control of your present and your future.

10 Steps to Investing in Your Life

1. Identify the areas of your life today that are not exactly and perfectly the way you want them to be.
2. Sort these into major categories such as physical, emotional, intellectual, academic, job-related, relational, spiritual, and so on.
3. Prioritize your list and determine which way to approach it.
   a. What one item in each area can I do something (small or big) about right now?
   b. What area, and all things listed in this area, will I make a major investment in?
4. Understand that "investment" can mean money, time, energy, emotion, passion, or even just the thought space required.
5. Determine the minimums and maximums of your investments (in all the areas). What *can* you invest? What are you unwilling to invest?
6. Understand that often investments can create reduced resources in certain areas. For example, when you buy stock as an investment, your cash flow is reduced. More time invested in one area reduces time left for other areas. Determine what real cost would be involved in any investment, and whether you are comfortable with this reality.
7. Understand that investments are made to yield profitable returns.
8. Evaluate your investments periodically for profitable return. Some investments may not yield the desired return. What will you do about this?
9. Commit to making investment in yourself a lifelong habit.
10. Focus your self-investments for greater return. You can have a "diverse portfolio," but this may limit the amount of return on any given investment.

Area A: Your Abilities and Skills to Earn Money

Identify five skills or abilities that you would benefit greatly from investing time, money, and energy in. Identify your reasons for desiring these skills, how you will develop them (who, what, where) and how much of a financial commitment (budget) you are willing and able to invest in this pursuit. Complete the following table.

Skill Investment Plan				
Desired Skill	Reasons	Time Commitment	Financial Commitment	Method

Now prioritize this list.

1. _____

2. _____

3. _____

4. _____

5. _____

Now pick the one you want to focus your investment on over the next 30 days and enter it here:

My top skill investment: _____

Make plans for all five on your list, after you have actually invested in your top desired skill.

A B C

Credit ⬤ ◯ ◯

When you have arranged for this skill investment/training, give yourself credit by filling in **Area A** of this lesson on the Personal Foundation Chart.

Area B: Your Advanced Personal Development

Identify the one major area of your personal development that you would benefit greatly from investing time, money, and energy in. Identify your reasons for choosing this area, how you will develop it (who, what, where), and how much of a financial commitment (budget) you are willing and able to invest in this pursuit. Complete the following table.

Personal Development Investment Plan	
Personal development area	
Why this area?	
Time commitment	
Financial commitment	
Method of development	
When will I start, and when will I stop?	
Evidence: *How* **will I know when I have completed this investment?**	

Credit

A B C

When you have been engaged in this focus for 90 days, give yourself credit by filling in **Area B** of this lesson on the Personal Foundation Chart.

Area C: High Quality of Life

Part 1: Today

Identify five "investments" you can make right now in order to make today better and ensure the highest quality of life for you at this time. These may include (large or small) things like more sleep, better eating habits, exercise, good reading, a new bed, or a personal organizer, and so on.

1. _____

2. _____

3. _____

4. _____

5. _____

Now, do it!

Part 2: Tomorrow

Identify five investments you can make right now, or in the future, that will benefit your tomorrow, and yield a higher quality of life. Check the appropriate time box.

High Quality of Life Investment Plan				
Investment	**Within 30 days**	**Within 6 months**	**Within 1 year**	**Within 5 years**

Part 3: A Big Change

What one thing can you invest in right now that will give you continued returns from this moment on and significantly increase your quality of life or perpetuate your current high quality of life?

The big one:_____

Credit

A B C
○ ○ ◉

When you have completed the tables in parts one and two and made the "big" change, give yourself credit by filling in **Area C** of this lesson on the Personal Foundation Chart.

Congratulations! Be ready for continuing high yields on your investments.

Choose Your Work to Be You

Key Points

- Work can meet many needs, including personal and lifestyle.
- Your life's work can bring out all of your gifts.
- Life's work is usually a synthesis of your key values.
- Work becomes something else when it causes pain.
- It takes time to discover and be your life's work.

Introduction

This is a design-it-yourself lesson. Only you can ask the right questions, make the right choices and take the right actions regarding your life work. You will be asked to complete every section of this lesson, in a similar format as others in the personal foundation program. Follow the instructions under each standard heading. For many of these sections you may need to use additional paper, or even a journal, in order to adequately complete this lesson.

Any work that you do can be a full expression of who you are today. Finding your life's work makes you more of who you are . . . forever.

Ask Yourself:

- How satisfying is my job?
- Does my job or career path have a real future, or is it fading?
- Does my work express my personal values?
- Is my work a form of play for me?
- Is there a standard career for me, or do I need to invent a niche or profession?
- Am I an entrepreneur, technician, or sales type of personality?
- How much does money, salary, or earnings play in my choice of work?
- What skills would it be wise to get or upgrade now in order to attract a better job?
- What is standing in the way of my success at work today?

Coaching Tips

○ How would you coach yourself, or others, regarding life work? Make several statements in the space provided that would be relevant for the coaching process in this lesson.

How do I coach myself or others in life work?

1. _____

_____

_____

_____

_____

_____

2. _____

_____

_____

_____

_____

_____

3. _____

_____

_____

_____

_____

4. _____

_____

_____

_____

_____

5. _____

_____

_____

_____

_____

Understanding Life Work

What information would you offer, reference, or recommend to help you or others understand life work and its importance in personal foundation? Provide that information, list reference sources, give clarifying explanations, and so on.

_____

_____

_____

_____

_____

_____

_____

_____

_____

_____

_____

_____

_____

_____

_____

_____

_____

_____

_____

_____

_____

_____

_____

_____

Benefits of Having Your Life Work Be You

List what the benefits would be for you to have your life work be who you are.

_____

_____

_____

_____

_____

10 Steps to Choosing a Life Work to Be You

What steps would _you_ take to make your life work be you? Make these simple, doable, and briefly stated.

1. _____

2. _____

3. _____

4. _____

5. _____

6. _____

7. _____

8. _____

9. _____

10. _____

Do-It-Yourself Area Mini-Projects

Determine three parts or areas for action and design three mini-projects, using the formats and ideas from previous lessons, which will strengthen your personal foundation in the area of life work. Be sure to give yourself credit on the Personal Foundation Chart when each area is complete. We have allowed one page for each area project (A, B, C). Ask questions, design personal worksheets, or do whatever is necessary to complete these projects. Give each area a title.

Area A:

_____

_____

_____

_____

_____

_____

_____

_____

_____

_____

A   B   C

Credit ◉ ○ ○

When you have designed and completed this project, give yourself credit by filling in **Area A** of this lesson on the Personal Foundation Chart.

Area B:

_____

_____

_____

_____

_____

_____

_____

_____

_____

_____

Credit A **B** C ○ ● ○
When you have designed and completed this project, give yourself credit by filling in **Area B** of this lesson on the Personal Foundation Chart.

Area C:

_____

_____

_____

_____

_____

_____

_____

_____

_____

Credit A B **C** ○ ○ ●
When you have designed and completed this project, give yourself credit by filling in **Area C** of this lesson on the Personal Foundation Chart.

Congratulations! **Well done!**

Choose a Healthy Attitude

Key Points

- Your attitude is your choice.
- Your personality may affect your attitude, but attitude is still a choice.
- Your situation may affect your attitude, but attitude is still a choice.
- Circumstances may affect your attitude, but attitude is still a choice.
- Choosing a healthy attitude is a habit that requires practice, but eventually becomes natural—regardless of personality, situation, or circumstances.
- A healthy attitude cultivates life fulfillment.

Introduction

Attitude is defined as a general feeling, manner of thinking, or disposition. Healthy, for the purposes of this lesson, is defined as a state of well-being. Quite often you characterize attitude as a way of thinking that falls on a scale whose low end is labeled "pessimistic" and whose high end is labeled "optimistic." It is the old adage of seeing a glass half full or half empty. Attitude is a life response mechanism. What you fail to realize in most cases, however, is that attitude is a choice. You choose how you respond to, and think about, certain specific events, circumstances, and situations, as well as life in general. A healthy attitude allows you to respond evenly, positively, and in balance and control at all times. The purpose of this lesson is to assist you in choosing the attitude that preserves your well-being.

Ask Yourself:

- What is my attitude most of the time?
- What usually affects my attitude in a negative way?
- What usually affects my attitude in a positive way?
- Am I prone to frequent attitude shifts and swings?
- What do others say about my attitude?
- Have I ever consciously chosen to shift my attitude? Has it worked?

Coaching Tips

Trying to dissect "attitude" can lead to various layers of complexities. What constitutes or evokes an attitude is difficult to determine. There are a number of components common to all attitudes including:

- Basic personality type
- Self-esteem
- Previous experiences
- Personal styles
- Situations and events
- Circumstances
- Physical and mental health
- Stress levels
- Values and beliefs

When you engage in personal development in the area of attitude, all of these components may come into play and may need to be honestly evaluated. Much of the work you are already doing in this program will most likely affect your overall attitude. However, while all of this is being viewed, it is vital to understand, again, that attitude is a choice, and you can consciously shift your attitude from one end of the scale to the other by degree or by whole sections. Your awareness of what constitutes your attitude can help greatly in making these shifts.

Making attitude shifts is not easy and will not come naturally without a great deal of initial desire, commitment, unrelenting practice, and the openness to learn about yourself. Attitude affects personal perception, and the process of consistently choosing a healthy attitude is greatly assisted by coaches and trusted friends to whom you give permission to be candid and hold you accountable in this effort. Without this support system, attitude adjustments and shifts will generally not succeed over the long term.

Understanding a Healthy Attitude

A number of the CoachInc.com Guiding Principles have tremendous relevance to this lesson and help you understand the basics of, and the need for, a healthy attitude. Once you understand the vital nature and role of attitude in your personal development, the commitment and desire to choose a healthy attitude is much stronger.

Guiding Principle 8 | **People Have a Choice.**
Awareness is the precursor to choice.

We have already discussed the fact that *attitude is a choice*. Unless an element of physical or mental illness is present, in which case you must seek the services of professionals trained in the healing of these areas, you are completely capable of choosing your attitude and deciding consciously whether it will be positive or negative.

Guiding Principle 5 | **People Seek Value.**
Connection is the wellspring of creativity.

A healthy attitude promotes value in our lives.
You have more opportunity to see and recognize value when your attitude is healthy. Knowing that all people seek value lets us pursue the concept that with a healthy attitude you can be open to receiving and recognizing more value—you consciously "listen" for it. You know that you shut down, to a certain extent, your receptors for positive things (things of value) when you have a bad attitude. And yes, there is such a thing as a bad attitude. A bad attitude is any attitude that keeps you from a state of well-being.

Guiding Principle 7 | **People Live From Their Perception.**
An inclusive, present-based perception of reality
is the platform for effective action.

A healthy attitude is discerning, open to opportunity, in spite of apparent circumstances.
Discernment is quickly clouded and confused by a less than healthy attitude. Your perception and ability to accurately discern truth, reality and opportunity is directly proportional to the vitality and health of your attitude. Perception and discernment are fused together, and both are dependent upon attitude. A healthy attitude opens the doors to perceiving opportunities, even in apparently negative situations, thereby obtaining value that could not otherwise be discerned.

Guiding Principle 4 | **People Grow from Connection.**
Connection is the wellspring of creativity.

A healthy attitude enhances our ability to connect with others and with creative opportunities.
Your attitude acts as a catalyst to either attract or repel connection. When your attitude is healthy, you are healthy, and can attract opportunities for connection, even in the middle of seemingly unpleasant or negative situations. It allows you to honestly and openly question, and to pursue answers, which lead to connections. A less than healthy attitude becomes a wall, separating you from these connections, closing the door. With a healthy attitude, you are more attractive.

Guiding Principle 2 | **People Are Inquisitive.**
Wonder, curiosity, and inquiry are the source of all learning.

A healthy attitude enhances learning.
When your attitudes are healthy, you are more inclined to wonder, to question why things happened as they did, to wonder how you can do things differently, and to learn from the past, and to be curious about what there is to learn in situations, circumstances, and life in general. A healthy attitude seeks the learning in all things. An unhealthy attitude restricts wonder, curbs curiosity and pretty much shuts down all inquiry. A pessimistic attitude is one of withdrawal, selfish and arrogant isolation, and deaf ears. The death of wonder and learning is a by-product of an unhealthy attitude.

The Numb Zone
In the middle of the attitude scale is the "numb zone." It has been given this name because it is lukewarm, without passion. This is no attitude at all and reflects nothingness. In the numb zone there is no wonder, and no curiosity, and therefore no inquiry. You may or may not perceive correctly, but you don't discern and you don't connect. The numb zone is an "I don't care" zone. Many people live there without even knowing it. The numb zone may be used, usually incorrectly and not honestly, as a protective place while you work on shifts and adjustments in attitude. On a linear scale, the numb zone must be passed on the way to the healthy end of the attitude scale. Some people will slide into this zone during these transitions, especially when shifting from the far end of the unhealthy side of

the scale. This place implies no emotion and no passion, which is a dangerous and usually dishonest place to reside. When choosing a healthy attitude, choose to leap over, rather than shift into, the numb zone. It is wise to keep this in mind when practicing this lesson!

Benefits of Choosing a Healthy Attitude

- Opportunities are much more obvious.
- Your state of well-being is more balanced and not subject to sudden change.
- Perception and discernment are dramatically enhanced.
- You become much more attractive and connect more often.
- Your life becomes less stressful and less difficult.

10 Steps to Choosing a Healthy Attitude

1. Understand that your attitude affects every area of your well-being (body, mind, and spirit).
2. Understand that you control your attitude. It is your choice.
3. Honestly, as much as possible, evaluate your attitudes over the long term and short term, in general and in specific situations.
4. Ask for the assistance of your coach and trusted friends to give you honest feedback about your attitudes. (You are not always able to honestly evaluate them, especially at the time they are experienced or exhibited.) What do they say about your attitude(s)? Do you agree or disagree?
5. Evaluate the influences that cause you to experience a positive disposition and those that elicit a negative disposition.
6. Determine how you can make choices to consciously change your attitude about things in general, and specific things.
7. Develop an "early warning" system that alerts you to the potential of unhealthy attitudes and decide ahead of time how you will cope with impending influences that may affect your attitude.
8. Make a commitment to monitor your attitude for a specific period of time, with the intent to make a choice for a healthy attitude. Evaluate your findings.
9. Give your coach and friends permission to hold you accountable and gently remind or alert you of unhealthy attitudes they observe in you.
10. Make a commitment to always choose to be positive, to be open to opportunities, and to control your attitude through conscious choice.

Area A: Attitude Influencers

We stated early in this lesson that there are many components to attitude. Some of these have combined over your lifetime to produce a certain general disposition or attitude about everything—life in general—not just specifics. Take the time to honestly evaluate some of these areas. Consider how the areas outlined in the following table may have influenced your attitude in the past. Write down specific incidents, conditions, realities, and experiences under each heading, then write how these things have shaped your attitude (in healthy or unhealthy ways).

General Attitude Profile	
Influence	**Affect on My Attitude**
My family	
My culture	
My values and beliefs	
My general background	
My specific experiences	
My education	
My personality style	
Other	

Are you able to put the things on this list aside, so that they do not affect your attitude in an unhealthy way? This does *not* mean that you abandon values and beliefs. It only means that your attitude is not adversely affected by them. Over the next 30 days consciously practice letting go of anything on this list that you observe dragging your attitude into the unhealthy end of the scale. Ask for help in monitoring this.

A B C

Credit ● ○ ○

When you have completed this list and have successfully been able to sustain a healthy attitude not affected by these things for 30 days, give yourself credit by filling in **Area A** of this lesson on the Personal Foundation Chart.

Area B: Transitioning to a Healthy Attitude

Having a healthy attitude is not about changing behavior. That would be the easy part. It is about changing how you *feel* about things, and it goes much deeper than surface behavior. You probably know yourself pretty well, and know when your attitude is less than healthy. Identify the situations, circumstances, and conditions that you know are your vulnerable places—things that cause you to respond with a less than healthy attitude. Write down how you usually feel about or respond to these things, and the choices you will make regarding attitude in the future.

Unhealthy Attitude Hot Spots		
Conditions, circumstances, situations	My past attitude/ response	My future attitude/ response choice

Chances are that at least one of these "hot spots" will be activated in the next 30 days. Practice making the choices you have indicated in your attitude about these things, consistently over the next month.

Credit A **B** C

When you have completed the table and have successfully made the choice to have a healthy attitude about the things on this list, give yourself credit by filling in **Area B** of this lesson on the Personal Foundation Chart.

Area C: Plan for a Healthy Attitude

Having a healthy attitude does not happen by itself. This is especially true if you are making great leaps from the unhealthy end of the scale or learning how to control great attitude swings. It requires a plan and a solid promise to yourself to practice and perfect having a healthy attitude. Take some time to develop a plan and complete the following.

1. Are you serious about having a healthy attitude? Are you willing to commit wholeheartedly to this? If so, write a brief statement that reflects your commitment:

_____

_____

_____

2. I have given permission to the following people to monitor and give me feedback about my attitude:

_____

_____

_____

3. What do you see as your biggest challenge in having a consistently healthy attitude?

_____

_____

_____

4. What is your plan for meeting this challenge?

_____

_____

_____

5. How will you keep yourself tuned in or alert to your attitude at any given time? How will you know when you need to make a choice to have a healthy attitude (instead of an unhealthy attitude) about something at any time? What reminders or systems (outside of other people's feedback) will work to keep you successfully monitoring your attitude? Ultimately, your healthy attitude must be an internal choice, not one stimulated by external means. How will you do this in the moment, and not after the fact? (This is your "early warning" system.)

_____

_____

_____

6. In addition to your personal "monitors," what other support will you use to help you make consistent choices for a healthy attitude? Other people? Faith? Reference sources? Reminders? Journaling? Be specific. You *will* need the support!

_____

_____

_____

7. Other (This is up to you. What else do you need for your plan?)

_____

_____

_____

A B **C**

Credit ◯◯● When you have completed the plan and have successfully implemented it for 30 days, with a noticeable and verifiable change in your choices about attitude, give yourself credit by filling in **Area C** of this lesson on the Personal Foundation Chart.

Congratulations! **You probably found this harder than you thought, but well worth the effort.** Choosing a healthy attitude will serve you well throughout your life. You will never regret it.

Create a Reserve

Key Points

- You need more than you think you need.
- A reserve is far, far more than you need.
- With a reserve, you are at choice.
- You can get a reserve in at least 10 areas.
- The process of creating a reserve strengthens you.

Introduction

To have a reserve means that you have more than you need, often so much more that you essentially have no needs. Having a reserve is having much more than you need in every area of your life: finances, time and rest, personal space, energy, and so on. In today's world, most people are running on fumes. The reserve tanks are empty. Your choices are so much easier and automatic with a reserve. All of life becomes easier, more natural.

Ask Yourself:

- Do I know what it means to have a reserve? Do I even understand this concept?
- How would it feel to have reserves in every area of my life?
- Can I have too much?
- When does a reserve become an obsession?
- How does a reserve keep itself maintained?
- What do I have to do?
- What is the level beyond a reserve for me?

Coaching Tips

- Building a reserve happens more easily when you have plugged the holes in your life, as described in the integrity, needs, boundaries, and other lessons.

- You are not acquiring a reserve as a thing separate from yourself. You are building yourself up as you acquire a reserve. A reserve is not just an external object—it also feeds you.

- You need a reserve more than you know you need a reserve. Just start the process and watch how easy your life gets and how free and able you feel. It works.

Understanding Reserves

With a reserve, you are at choice.

Because you have needs, your life choices are limited—one part of you is compelled to focus on what you need for survival, while the other part of you can go off and explore. The more your needs are handled (via reserves and other lessons), the more time you have to stretch and grow and the less time and space you spend being concerned about your survival.

With a strong reserve, you are truly at choice. This means that you can have what you want and need, spend your time doing what fulfills you, and truly be yourself. You can try to be yourself without a reserve, but it is rarely sustainable or consistent.

Creating a reserve will upgrade your systems.

Upgraded systems are a natural benefit of creating reserves. When you reach your reserves goal, you will have the systems in place to automatically protect and replenish your reserves. Consider the lottery winner who gets a $1,000,000 jackpot but spends, wastes, or invests it unwisely so that it all disappears in very little time. This happens frequently. Why? Because the winner has not developed the internal systems and degree of awareness and understanding to handle well what they have been given.

You need a reserve in 10 areas.

Reserves are needed in all of these areas of life:

1. *Time.* Having at least an hour or two of time each day, beyond resting, just for you.
2. *Space.* Having room to think and be, without pressure, obligation, or adrenaline.
3. *Money.* Having cash in the bank or solid investments to fund your present and future.
4. *Energy.* Having enough oomph to get through the day consistently and rest well at night.
5. *Opportunity.* Having enough good stuff coming at you so that you can trust the future.
6. *Love.* Having enough, and the right kind of, caring, support, and love from those who matter to you.
7. *Information.* Having access to all that you need to know to grow, succeed, perform, and work.
8. *Wisdom.* Having access to someone and some place where you can grow and develop yourself easily and naturally.
9. *Self.* Having more than enough of a relationship with yourself (knowing yourself).
10. *Integrity.* Living your life with higher than necessary standards, a high-quality lifestyle, wholeness, etc.

Benefits of Having Reserves

- Basic fears are eliminated.
- You have freedom from worries.
- Life becomes effortless.
- You become more attractive.
- You gain space to grow and be at peace.
- You have ease and comfort in emergencies.

10 Steps to Building Your Reserves

1. Understand completely that you need reserves.
2. Commit to building reserves. Make it a top priority.
3. Examine the 10 reserve areas and determine honestly what you have now, and what you need to be comfortable in the future. Comfortable means without worries.
4. Understand that building reserves is not about striving or stressing to do so. It is intended to become a part of your natural organization and purpose. It should not consume you.
5. Write out what you have observed as far as current and future reserve needs.
6. Think carefully through each of the 10 areas, and spend some time considering all your options for building adequate, or more than adequate, reserves. Don't write anything down until you have thought it all out well. Keep a list or idea page always available to jot down notes as you think of them.
7. Keep reserve building at the front of your daily thoughts. Get used to the idea and let it become natural. Consider your reserves and the concept of continually building in all the choices you make.
8. After careful thought, sit down and write out a plan for reserve building. How, in a practical and nonstressful way, will you build the reserves you need?
9. Try doubling what you think you need on your plan. What does this do to the plan? To your thoughts about this concept?
10. Now work your plan and relax.

Area A: Reserve Building Focus #1

Drawing from the 10 reserve areas listed.
Please select one area that would serve you well right now. Make sure it is the right time for the one you select. Do not select one that you *should* select. Select the one that you are ready to work on and succeed with. Enter it on the line immediately preceding and on the line indicated in the worksheet that follows.

Identify what the full level would be for what you wrote down, and make it measurable.
For example, if you selected a reserve of space, the full reserve level might be look like this:

- No problems
- No pressure
- Plenty of time to kick back and relax and be
- All the space I need to be very creative

Enter this information in the worksheet that follows.

Identify what is needed in order to build your reserve.
This may include action, changes, plugging holes, being attentive to your needs, acquiring assets, working harder, telling the truth, moving, changing jobs, mastering other lessons of the personal foundation program, and so on.

Identify any milestones, measurements, or markers.
Note any that will help you determine when you have reached *full* for this reserve.

Complete the following worksheet.

Reserve Building Worksheet		
Reserve Focus #1:		
Full Reserve Indicators (what this includes or looks like for you)	**Steps I Will Take to Build This Reserve**	**Milestones or Measurements to Determine Full Reserve**

A B C

Credit ●○○ When you have taken the actions and reached your full reserve level in this area, give yourself credit by filling in **Area A** of this lesson on the Personal Foundation Chart.

Area B: Reserve Building Focus #2

Refer to the steps outlined above in Area A, and choose another reserve focus. Write it in the line provided, and complete the following worksheet.

Reserve Building Worksheet		
Reserve Focus #2:		
Full Reserve Indicators (what this includes or looks like for you)	**Steps I Will Take to Build This Reserve**	**Milestones or Measurements to Determine Full Reserve**

A B C

Credit ○●○ When you have taken the actions and reached your full reserve level in this area, give yourself credit by filling in **Area B** of this lesson on the Personal Foundation Chart.

Area C: Reserve Building Focus #3

Refer to the steps outlined in Area A, and choose a third reserve focus. Write it in the line provided, and complete the following worksheet.

Reserve Building Worksheet		
Reserve Focus #3:		
Full Reserve Indicators (what this includes or looks like for you)	**Steps I Will Take to Build This Reserve**	**Milestones or Measurements to Determine Full Reserve**

Credit A B **C** ◯◯⬤

When you have taken the actions and reached your full reserve level in this area, give yourself credit by filling in **Area C** of this lesson on the Personal Foundation Chart.

You have made a great start here. See the Resources section of this module to acces a blank worksheet to help you build the remaining reserve areas. Keep it up!

Congratulations! Continue building your reserves. You will never be the same!

Start Attracting

Key Points

- Attraction is not promotion or seduction.
- To be attractive means that good things come to you.
- Adding value, relating well, and serving are attractive.
- When you have a reserve, you naturally attract.
- A "makeover" is usually needed to be fully attractive.
- Once you are attractive, self-promotion is not needed and in fact will not work anymore.

Introduction

As you develop, you prefer to become attractive to opportunities, yourself, others, potential customers, and the future, rather than becoming better at promoting, marketing, seducing, controlling, or manipulating. We call being very attractive irresistible attraction.

The purpose of this lesson is to let you focus on this idea and to determine three ways for you (personally, in your business, in your life, etc.) to become much more attractive. Attraction is a key part of your personal foundation.

Ask Yourself:

- Do others find me attractive? How do I know?
- How do I define attraction?
- Why should I become attractive?
- What people do I find attractive? Why?

Coaching Tips

○ The concept of attractiveness is not about working to achieve it. Understand that it comes naturally after other areas of your life are in harmony and you are completely living in integrity. The process of bringing all the pieces of your life into a wholeness and perfect interrelationship is a valuable lesson in itself. Each lesson serves as a part of the makeover you are doing on your life. Give each area the attention it needs and don't skip quickly to other areas until that part is complete. Remember, attractiveness will be increased with every step you make. Don't expect to work for it. It works for you.

Guiding Principle 4 | **People Grow from Connection.**
Connection is the wellspring of creativity.

Understanding Attraction

Attraction is the principle that once you make your life a problem-free zone, build up your reserves, live in integrity, choose a healthy attitude, and complete virtually every other lesson you have already worked through in this personal foundation program, you will no longer have to resort to promotion and seduction to accomplish what you want in life. You will not have to go hunt down or pursue the things you want—they will come to you. Through this path of self-development, through the personal foundation lessons, you become attractive to others and to opportunities. Attractive, in the sense we mean for this concept, does not mean physical beauty or a nice façade. It means inner beauty, inner peace, inner contentment, and wholeness that naturally attracts, draws, and entices into your life what you have been previously striving for.

In Guiding Principle #6, people do grow from connection. Attraction is the portal to connection. Connections cannot be formed unless attraction has occurred first. Attraction cannot be manufactured or produced by your work. It is a quality, a by-product of living in integrity—being whole in every way. The lessons you have already completed, if done completely and with the commitment to maintain them, will produce the quality of attraction in your life. The following steps should, by now, be natural for you, and all contribute to attraction.

Show that you care.
Be able to touch someone emotionally, yet professionally, if appropriate. We all need a special connection. Want a lot for others, perhaps even more than they want for themselves. Then share it. Tell people who they are, not just what they do; remind them if necessary. People forget.

Be somebody.
Master your craft to the point where you are innovating and exciting. Keep it up. Be an adult. Resolve the problems and concerns you have, and then become a problem-free zone. Be on a strong personal path so that you have a well-balanced life today and a great future. Being somebody does not mean achievement or advancement in career or rank of some sort. It means *being* who you are, not pretending to be someone else or wishing you were someone else.

Be able to "dance."
"Hear it all," even what others have not said. The more you listen and genuinely hear, the more you partner with that person. Ask the right questions, especially the ones, that reorient and develop others, helping them see things previously unseen. When you respond and speak, make sure your words contain the right messages. Package what you say so that others are motivated to respond well. Have no expectations and know how to "dance" in situations and circumstances that require flexibility and understanding.

Advance the action.
Be unconditionally constructive in every communication, with every person. Say nothing but the very best. Speak "charge neutral." You can say anything to anyone when there is no charge (condemnation, accusation, anger, tone, etc.) in your voice. Be sure that all you say and do with others is consciously designed to advance them.

Deliver.
Underpromise, even underpromise what you know you can deliver. Deliver 20% more. Anticipate and deliver more than what is needed. Fulfill the needs others have not thought of yet. Stay ahead of them. This simple action says loudly that you care. In your business, open up conversations for service in areas the client has not yet asked for. Create demand, and then meet it beyond expectations.

Have a community.

Have a strong professional network spanning 50 fields of expertise, if possible. Have resources. Be close to your natural family or family of choice. They give you the strength you need. Have strong and supportive friendships. Enjoy people. Expect less and give more.

Be a model.

Set and live up to very high personal standards, the ones you know you truly want. Have extensive boundaries so you are insulated from other people's problems. Be "present perfect": Have everything and everyone around you be in great shape. Live the way you want to be known and the way you want others to live.

These are only a small sample of the countless ways you can become attractive. Every lesson in this program is designed to deliver the ultimate benefit of making you more attractive to others.

Benefits of Being Attractive

- Good things come to you without your trying to grab them for yourself.
- You will no longer need to practice self-promotion or "seductive" techniques to get noticed, get business, or get anything else for that matter.
- You have much less stress and frenzy through life.
- You gain a sense of peace and contentedness (those things in themselves are attractive).

10 Steps to Becoming Attractive

1. Understand that this list is not about doing, but being.
2. Complete every lesson in the Personal Foundation program.
3. Eliminate every self-promotional activity you engage in now.
4. Working from the previous list, show that you care.
5. Be somebody—*you*.
6. Be flexible and dance well.
7. Advance the action; always be constructive and motivating.
8. Deliver more than expected. Expect less.
9. Have a community and contribute; don't just take.
10. Be a model.

Area A: Attraction Focus #1

Select or adapt an area to work on from the foregoing list or choose another area that you know will make you much more attractive in your life. Write the focus title on the line provided and in the worksheet that follows. Identify three things you can *do* or *be* to make yourself more attractive. Indicate how not just doing but *being* these things or ways will make you more attractive. Consider both professional and personal issues. Complete the worksheet, and then incorporate these points into the overall integrity of who you are and *how* you act.

Attraction Worksheet

Attraction Focus #1:

	Things I can DO, or ways I can BE	How this will enhance my attractiveness
1.		
2.		
3.		

A B C
Credit ● ○ ○

When you have implemented these three items, give yourself credit by filling in **Area A** of this lesson on the Personal Foundation Chart.

Area B: Attraction Focus #2

Do the same as you did in Area A, following the same instructions, only this time choose another area of focus. Write it on the line provided, and complete the following worksheet.

Attraction Worksheet

Attraction Focus #2:

	Things I can DO, or ways I can BE	How this will enhance my attractiveness
1.		
2.		
3.		

Credit

A **B** C
○ ● ○

When you have implemented these three items, give yourself credit by filling in **Area B** of this lesson on the Personal Foundation Chart.

Area C: Attraction Focus #3

Do the same as you did in Area A, following the same instructions, only this time choose a third area of focus. Write it on the line provided, and complete the following worksheet.

Attraction Worksheet		
Attraction Focus #3:		
	Things I can DO, or ways I can BE	**How this will enhance my attractiveness**
1.		
2.		
3.		

Credit

A B **C**
○ ○ ●

When you have implemented these three items, give yourself credit by filling in **Area C** of this lesson on the Personal Foundation Chart.

Congratulations! Enjoy your new level of attractiveness!

Perfect the Present

Key Points

- When you can view the present as perfect, you can begin to see how other things, including you, are perfect too.
- You may not like the present, but it's still perfect.
- The perfection of the present may not be what you prefer.
- You can always improve the present, but it's perfect.
- When the present is perfect for you, celebrate.

Introduction

Many of us are either driven to create a fabulous future for ourselves or focused on spending a lifetime in our quest to resolve the issues that affect and limit us. There is nothing wrong with either of these approaches, but there is a limitation to our accomplishment with this orientation.

The limitation is that neither is about the present moment—both are about a different time. It is worthwhile to go into the past and to visualize the future, but only when done with both feet firmly in a healthy present.

What is the present? The present is simply the reality of your life as it is today. The present is what is so right now. Not what could be so, and should or shouldn't be so, but actually what IS so—whether you like it or not. There is a richness in the present, and when understood, this fact puts the past and the future in the proper light.

Coaching Tips

○ **The Present *is* Perfect.**
The way things are today is that way for a good reason (even if you can't see or understand the reason). It is a lesson just to understand that the present is perfect. This means giving up how things were, could be, should be, or need to be.

○ **When you perfect what you already have, you will attract more.**
When you live well with all you have been given, you see you have it all. And when you are in this space, you will attract more of what you want. You can't fake being in this space, nor can you strive to create this space. Basically, you have to give up the future, focus on today, perfect today, and enjoy it. The next opportunity will occur.

○ **Start with today.**
Rather than setting goals about the future (more money, success, clients, etc.), it usually works best to set goals for the present. For instance, how are you doing today—what do you have around that is just waiting for some attention? Which opportunities are patiently waiting for you to hear them? To perfect the present means to make today perfect—not just say it, but make it. Go out and make the present perfect . . . and enjoy it.

○ **You can still want, and go for, more.**
Understanding that the present is perfect doesn't mean you can't have more of a good thing! It just means you can start creating the next goal from a healthier place.

Benefits of Perfecting the Present

- You can ignore the future.
- You get pleasure immediately instead of waiting for a goal to be reached.
- You experience greater awareness of yourself.
- You are aligning yourself with what is so, and not what should be, was or could be. This can set you free.

Guiding Principle 7 | **People Live from Their Perception.**
An inclusive, present-based perception of reality
is the platform for effective action.

Area A: Perfect Yesterday

The assignment is to make yesterday perfect. It's true, you are supposed to be working on the present—as in today—but today is very much today because of how yesterday was or in what shape you left yesterday.

On the following lines, go back in your mind and write down the 10 things about yesterday that you did not leave perfect. Now, go ahead and take an hour, or less, to perfect yesterday.

To Perfect Yesterday:

1. _____

2. _____

3. _____

4. _____

5. _____

6. _____

7. _____

8. _____

9. _____

10. _____

Credit

A B C

When you have written down and perfected the 10 items from yesterday, give yourself credit by filling in **Area A** of the lesson on the Personal Foundation Chart.

Area B: Understand Today IS Perfect

This assignment differs from the previous one in that you won't be *doing* anything about today, only understanding that it is perfect.

On the lines below, write down the five things that are clearly *not* perfect about today or your life. Then, study each one and write down how it *is* perfect, even if it's 180 degrees from how you want it. Take your time. *See* the perfection of it instead of "trying to make it perfect in your mind." Today *is* perfect. Stick with it until you get it, like when viewing those 3D posters that require you to relax your eyes so that the third dimension pops out at you clearly. The image is always there—you just couldn't see it.

The Item That Isn't Perfect	How It Is Perfect
1.	
2.	
3.	
4.	
5.	

Credit

A **B** C

When you have written down the five "not perfects" of today and have come to see how they truly are perfect, give yourself credit by filling in **Area B** of this lesson on the Personal Foundation Chart.

Area C: Make Tomorrow Perfect

This assignment is more like the first one of this lesson. Look ahead to tomorrow and make tomorrow perfect, even before it happens. What is going on tomorrow that you can do something about and perfect today, so that when it happens tomorrow, it is truly perfect? Go for it! List five things about tomorrow and what you can do today on the following lines.

	The Items Occurring Tomorrow	How To Perfect Them Today
1.		
2.		
3.		
4.		
5.		

Credit

A B **C**

When you have perfected tomorrow, today, give yourself credit by filling in **Area C** of this lesson on the Personal Foundation Chart.

Guiding Principle 6 | **People Act in Their Own Best Interest.**
Discernment reveals the opportunities in every situation.

25 Secrets to Having the Life You Want

These are simple to learn, though not necessarily easy to achieve.

○ You will accomplish much more, much more easily if you take the time to first strengthen your personal foundation.
○ Come to see how perfect your life is today, even if it doesn't look or feel that way.
○ Proactively choose the type of energy that you want to use during your life.
○ Decide that you want to learn, continuously and forever. Then choose to learn how to learn.
○ Reorient your life around the gifts you have, no matter what they are.
○ Put your integrity first, your needs second, and your wants third.
○ Let yourself have it all, even if it feels like too much.
○ Before you create a future, resolve the past and perfect the present.
○ For an effortless life, get more than you need and far more than you deserve.
○ Invest 10 percent of your time in maximizing the other 90 percent.
○ Set your goals based on your values, not on coulds, woulds, wills, or shoulds.
○ Start on your path to financial independence even if it doesn't seem realistic.
○ Stop trying to change your behavior; instead, start shifting and evolving.
○ Triple your personal boundaries until your heart and spirit have the room they need.
○ Stop hanging around people who have less to lose than you do.
○ Stop waiting for anything. Instead, initiate 100 percent of the time.
○ Solve your problems, even if you didn't cause them.
○ Build a community of people who bring out your best without trying to.
○ Develop your spirituality in a way that feels right to you.
○ Educate your environment until it responds to you the way you like.
○ Have more than enough love in your life.
○ Let your vision set your goals and guide your life.
○ Expand your vocabulary so you can be and share yourself.
○ Get comfortable with change and chaos.
○ Get a coach.

200+ Tolerations

Here's an idea list of things to stop tolerating.

- ○ Not enough storage space for all my office files
- ○ A desk full of stacks of papers
- ○ Peeling wallpaper
- ○ A partner who is not unconditionally constructive with my child or children
- ○ Being overweight
- ○ A web page that needs updating
- ○ Hair that doesn't look good
- ○ A guest bedroom that needs cleaning up (it looks like a storage room)
- ○ A partner's messy office
- ○ A kitchen that needs a dishwasher (and it shouldn't be me)
- ○ Not enough time scheduled for dreaming
- ○ Not enough time spent in the garden
- ○ Not setting time aside to meditate
- ○ Not saving money every month
- ○ Not getting paid on time by all of my clients
- ○ Clients who cancel appointments at the last moment
- ○ Excessive clutter
- ○ Storage shed that is so full you can't get into it
- ○ Investments that should be reevaluated but haven't been
- ○ Needing a water purifyer
- ○ Solar panels on the roof that need fixing
- ○ House walls that need painting
- ○ Kitchen floor that needs new tile
- ○ Not having a spare key for the car
- ○ Not having a well pump for the well
- ○ The fact that I must park four blocks from work
- ○ The no-leadership style of my boss
- ○ A half-finished kitchen
- ○ Tripping over my dog's toys throughout the house
- ○ Having to get up each morning before the sun rises
- ○ Evening telephone solicitations
- ○ Limited trunk space in my car
- ○ Mortgage and car payments
- ○ Negative attitudes of people with whom I work
- ○ Needy relatives
- ○ Poor customer service and inadequate responses from vendors
- ○ Eating too much sugar and salt
- ○ Low levels of reserves
- ○ Too many possessions that need to be cleaned
- ○ A backyard that is an eyesore

○ A constant need for home maintenance and repairs
○ The invasiveness of e-mail and the Internet
○ People or institutions that don't return my calls
○ My lack of creative outlet
○ Being part of a profession whose goals and standards I can no longer relate to
○ Knowing all my debt will not be paid off for another 10 years
○ Inadequate retirement fund
○ Demands on my time by my children
○ A former spouse who does not contribute time or money to raising our children
○ The insanity of television newscasts
○ Not having replacement belts for my vacuum cleaner
○ Mildew in the grout of the tiles in my shower
○ Mildew on the plastic shower curtain
○ A crack in the sealer around the base of the shower
○ The outdated or broken tile in the bathroom
○ Missing lights on the medicine cabinet
○ Spiderwebs in the corners
○ Stuff on top of my fridge that has not been put away since I had that Christmas party 10 years ago
○ The dog hair that shows up somewhere else the minute I clean it up
○ Keeping the end table by my chair cluttered in order to put my coffee cup on it because if it's cleaned off the cat will lie on it, leaving no room for my coffee cup
○ Cat food on the kitchen table because it's the only surface the dog won't get to
○ New slipcovers that aren't quite the right shade
○ An area rug that doesn't match the living room
○ Thirty-year-old wall-to-wall carpeting that resists cleaning attempts
○ A dining room table currently covered with stuff not related to dining
○ Whites that have yellowed because of hard water
○ A humidifier that needs a new filter to work properly
○ An inherited chest of drawers that has a broken piece of veneer
○ Fixing one toleration by putting up a window shade only to have it become a new toleration because it doesn't fit properly
○ A cat that lies on my wrists when I'm working on the computer
○ A living room window that is cracked and so dirty I can't see out of it when the sun is shining
○ Having a nice attic but not being able to get into it because the steps are falling apart
○ Cleaning supplies that won't fit under the sink
○ Spending eight hours a day in a room with no window
○ A coworker who has more tolerations than I do and spends all day talking about them
○ Being the office dumping ground because I'm such a good listener
○ Having a sugar and caffeine addiction
○ Taking antidepressants and experiencing more severe PMS symptoms than before
○ Taking antidepressants and gaining weight because I can't seem to care about changing my eating habits any more
○ Wearing only what's comfortable even if I don't like the way I look
○ Squirrels getting in the bird feeder
○ Having gotten very good at acting patient and hating every minute of it

- Not making time for art or music or crafts
- Water stains on the walls
- A roof that is only half reshingled
- Rusty iron porch railings
- Trim on the house that needs to be painted
- House that needs to be repainted
- Being deep in debt with no end in sight
- Not having a coach because I can't afford one
- Not being able to do much about most of my tolerations because they need money to be resolved
- Not having a nice stereo
- Having a saddle and riding boots and no horse
- Loving to travel and not knowing when I'll next be able to take a trip somewhere
- Not being able to come up with a concrete way to describe what I'm doing as a coach
- Having so many talents and interests that I'm constantly being pulled in lots of directions
- Being very good at maintaining acquaintances but having few close friends
- Not knowing how to build a network or not being able to figure it out in a way that isn't too overwhelming
- Being easily overwhelmed and trying to act like I'm not
- Being surrounded by people that think following your dreams is a needless, self-indulgent activity
- Throwing away money on things I don't really need or use
- Being from and living in a community where it's ingrained in the collective consciousness that the more you're tolerating, the more righteous you are
- Hating the way animals are processed for food and yet not being able to give up eating beef because it's comfort food
- Fearing that if I move to someplace I love to visit, it will be ruined forever
- Knowing that I'm the only reliable sibling and that when the time comes that my parents need to be cared for, it's all going to fall on me
- Knowing I can't afford to move anywhere even if I wanted to
- Knowing that techniques like affirmations, self-hypnosis, and guided imagery work for me but still not practicing them
- Not having 20 clients that are like my one wonderful client who will pay me $200 a month (or more)
- Not having a garage for my car
- Large parts of my lawn being covered in weeds
- Writing a volunteer weekly column for the local newspaper for months, wanting to be paid for it now, and not knowing what to do about it
- The fact that my laptop computer has needed a new battery for months
- Having boxes of things that need to be donated but that I haven't taken to the donation center
- Being so intent on being true to myself that it gets in my way
- Not having enough time to read and understand all that I want to
- Believing things that people say when I know they are not true for me
- Spending 95 percent of my waking hours struggling with frustration of some sort or another
- Being hungry but not wanting to stop what I am doing to get something to eat
- Having more books than bookshelves

○ Working at a job I don't enjoy
○ Having friends who are almost all 10 to 20 years older than I am
○ Not knowing how to ask for space from people without getting snippy because I've waited too long to ask
○ Having health insurance that doesn't pay for massage therapy or other alternative therapies
○ Having lower back problems from sitting in a nonergonomic chair all day
○ Having one of those combination copier/scanner/answering/fax machines when all I really need is a flatbed scanner
○ Having someone in my life who always tries to tell me what to do
○ Not knowing how to tell someone in my life to stop hurting my feelings without hurting his or her feelings
○ Feeling that if my parents died tomorrow, it would be catastrophic for me, even though I think I've been trying to plan ahead
○ Living in an uninsulated house in a place where it gets really hot or really cold
○ Being designated the keeper of the peace in the family
○ Being really sentimental
○ Having a poorly designed kitchen
○ Having a neat-looking 1950s stove or oven, only part of which works
○ Being crabby a lot
○ Not having a friend in the same town that I can just call up on the spur of the moment to go out with to do something
○ Feeling like I don't really have time to things that are just for fun
○ Living too far away from places I enjoy visiting: museums, specialty shops, like-minded organizations, but not wanting to move
○ Living with a constant inner sense of deep frustration
○ The lack of sunlight in winter
○ Fear of ice on the sidewalks
○ Living in a dangerous area
○ Beating myself up because I can't seem to apply all the things I know to myself
○ Not getting enough deep belly laughing every day
○ Having brains and talent but not knowing of any means of making a living from them
○ Feeling victimized and helpless and hating myself when I see others being victims too
○ Experiencing lots of synchronicity with tiny things every day, but not with the big important things
○ Not having a life plan that seems doable
○ Forty-year-old carpet in my bedroom and a mismatched bedroom set
○ The pile of stuff on top of the dresser that I can't seem to throw away
○ Not having organized Christmas decorations
○ A brown splotch on the wall from where I killed an insect
○ Having insects show up every now and then high on my bedroom walls where I can't reach them
○ Having insect invasions every summer
○ Visible dust collected on the top of the ceiling fan in the bedroom
○ Not being able to see my clock or radio without my glasses
○ A partner who chews food noisily
○ A partner who hates where we live
○ No table light in my bedroom

- No reserve of income
- Not taking a holiday every year
- Not visiting friends or family as often as I'd like to
- Having old, worn-out shoes
- A car that needs washing
- A back bumper that needs replacing
- Clothing of dissatisfying quality
- Living on a noisy main road
- Not having a strong community
- No recreation in my life
- Not going dancing regularly
- Underselling myself
- Shelves waiting to go up
- New light fittings waiting to go up
- Cupboard door hanging off
- Sock drawer broken
- Upstairs room still waiting to be upgraded
- A kitchen that has room only for one person at a time
- Carpet that needs cleaning
- Insufficient income
- Few visitors to the house
- Weak networks
- No fun opportunities
- Credit card debt
- Lack of discipline in myself
- An echo in my phone line
- My spouse's tone of voice with me
- A client who changes appointments frequently
- Too much e-mail
- Clothing that doesn't complement my body shape
- My frying pan–everything sticks
- My phone headset that doesn't fit my head or ear properly
- A lack of consistent income
- Telemarketing calls at inconvenient times
- Cell phone battery that needs replacing
- A stock of magazines and not enough time to read them
- A lack of support in my local professional group
- My tenant's late rent payments
- A lack of closet space in my home
- Too much television
- A lack of communication with my spouse
- Too much paperwork.
- A lack of an up-to-date business plan
- Fleas on my pets
- A lack of clients
- Software that doesn't work
- A messy studio/home/bedroom/other room
- A web site that doesn't reflect me
- Dandruff
- Cooking dinner every night when I don't want to

○ People who go beyond the bounds of decency
○ A dent in the front door of my car
○ An overcrowded filing cabinet
○ Not having a car I enjoy driving
○ Feeling depressed and not taking enough action
○ Dissatisfaction with my sexual relationship with my partner
○ Unsorted boxes of stuff in my closet
○ Holding on to clothes I don't really like
○ Gophers tunneling under my new front lawn
○ Termite damage to my house
○ A floor that needs refinishing
○ A broken sun visor in my car
○ Holding on to some stocks that have lost me a lot of money
○ My fear of analyzing my investments and taking the steps I need to get on the right track
○ Doing without an office assistant even though I need one
○ Not getting enough sleep to feel rested
○ My attitude that I should be able to handle everything on my own, even though I can't
○ People who criticize me
○ Not making enough money to afford what I want
○ A garage so full of stuff I can hardly move around in it
○ Windows that need cleaning
○ A garden shed that is rusting and needs replacing
○ Mildew on my roses
○ Lack of flowers in front of the house
○ Bedroom furniture that is no longer up to my standards
○ A backyard that needs landscaping
○ Not working out at least three times a week
○ A neighbor's pet that poops in my yard

25 Steps to a Strong Personal Foundation

These steps are based on the Personal Foundation program.

○ Decide that you want a strong personal foundation.
○ A strong foundation is a choice. Want it.
○ Zap the tolerations.
○ Whatever you are putting up with eats away at your personal foundation.
○ Simplify your life dramatically.
○ Resolve unfinished business.
○ Identify and focus on your 10 daily habits.
○ Restore your integrity wherever it's broken.
○ Get your needs met. You can.
○ Handle the money. Period.
○ Treat your body like the temple it is.
○ Extend your boundaries until you are fully respected.
○ Raise your standards until you feel terrific.
○ Create reserves in all areas of your life.
○ Perfect the present, especially if it's not.
○ Strengthen your family. Heal if necessary.
○ Extend your community.
○ Start attracting instead of striving.
○ Select and reach your preferred living states.
○ Be well protected.
○ Choose your work so that you can be all of yourself.
○ Reorient your life around your values.
○ Become a problem-free zone.
○ Improve your attitude.
○ Invest in your life.
○ Thank the people who've made your life as rich as it is.
○ Choose your postfoundation steps.

Reserve Index Program

Having a strong reserve in the six areas of your life is an advanced step in your personal development process. In fact, you are much more able to discover and share your unique gift when this reserve has been established.

The **Reserve Index** consists of 100 items that, when achieved, give you the inner strength you want because you then will have more than you need, personally and professionally.

The index is designed to be used in conjunction with the Reserve program or with your professional coach.

Benefits

On the lines provided, jot down specific benefits, results, and shifts that happened in your life because you handled an item in the Reserve Index.

Date	Benefit
_____	_____
_____	_____
_____	_____
_____	_____
_____	_____
_____	_____
_____	_____

Instructions

There are five steps to completing the Reserve Index.

Step 1: Answer each question.

If true, check the circle marked true. Be rigorous; be a hard grader. If the statement is sometimes or usually true, please do not check the circle until the statement is virtually always true for you; you get no credit until it is really true. If the statement does not apply to you, check the circle. If the statement will never be true for you, check the circle. You get credit for it because it does not apply or will never happen. You may also change any statement to fit your situation better.

Step 2: Summarize each section.

Add up the number of checked circles for each of the six sections and write those amounts where indicated. Then add up all six sections and write the total in the progress chart provided.

Step 3: Fill out the bonus section.

Please fill in the specific things or areas in which you do not currently have a reserve but know you really want one in. Select ones that are not mentioned in the other 90 choices.

Step 4: Color in the checklist provided.

If you have nine checks in the Time and Space section, for example, color in the bottom nine boxes of column A, and so on. Always work from the bottom up. The goal is to have all sections filled in. In the meantime, you have a current picture of how you are doing in each of the six areas.

Step 5: Keep playing until all boxes are filled in.

You can do it! This process may take 30 or 360 days, but you can achieve a perfect score on the Reserve Index. Use your coach or a friend to assist you. And check back once a year for maintenance.

Progress Chart

Date	Points (+/–)	Score

Reserve Index Program 100-Point Checklist

#	A	B	C	D	E	F	G
				Sections			
15							
14							
13							
12							
11							
10							
9							
8							
7							
6							
5							
4							
3							
2							
1							
2							
1							

Give yourself credit as you get points on the 100-point program. Fill in columns from the bottom up.

Special Note

If your total score starts out at 20 or 30 out of 100, don't worry about it. This is a rigorous list, and it takes time and training to reach 100.

We feel it is worth devoting time and energy to this process: Doing whatever it takes to be at 100 on this index strengthens you so you can afford (financially, personally, and professionally) to develop and share the unique and special gift you are.

A. Time and Space

Number of circles checked (15 max) _____

○ My gas tank is always at least half full.
○ I don't do errands, ever.
○ I am completely free of anything that binds me.
○ I am always 10 minutes early and never rushed.
○ My closets are empty of all that I don't need now.
○ I always wear a seat belt.
○ All my clothes are pressed or at the cleaners.
○ My three key boundaries are always honored.
○ The first and last 30 minutes of my day are the perfect way to arise and retire.
○ I don't get stopped or off track for more than one hour.
○ I am free of all addictions and attachments.
○ I have a daily routine that is a joy.
○ I use a time management system, and I do not miss appointments or forget things.
○ I do not tailgate, run yellow lights, or exceed the speed limit. I always let other cars in.
○ I do not do my own laundry or housework.

B. Love and Attraction

Number of circles checked (15 max) _____

○ No one in my life thinks I should change.
○ I received 25 cards on my last birthday.
○ My circle of 10 closest friends are fully supported and loved.
○ I grant everyone I know and everyone I've never met a lifetime of absolute forgiveness.
○ I have received 10 letters of gratefulness from friends or colleagues in the last 90 days.
○ I attract people rather than going after them.
○ I know the 10 things I want for others.
○ I speak straight, always and appropriately. I don't hold back—even on the little stuff.
○ I am a key part of a community of like-minded people.
○ I do not react to people; I have lots of space.
○ I treat everyone extremely well, from clerk to spouse.
○ I put my relationships far ahead of results.
○ I can afford to have others be right; they are.
○ I have no expectations (no hidden needs) of my friends and family—I expect nothing from them.
○ I've given a personal and extraordinary gift to my circle of 10 in the last six months.

C. Money and Freedom

Number of circles checked (15 max) _____

- ○ I always have $100 in my pocket that I never use.
- ○ I save or invest 20 percent of what I make each month.
- ○ I invest 5 percent of my revenue in my own training.
- ○ I have one year's reserve that I don't touch.
- ○ I have six months' worth of household and office supplies.
- ○ I charge more for my services than I think I am worth.
- ○ I am earning a stream of passive income.
- ○ I know how much I need to retire or be financially independent and am on that plan.
- ○ I have no credit card debt or short-term debt.
- ○ I make extra principal payments on my mortgage.
- ○ I keep at least $5,000 in my checking account.
- ○ I pay the full training tuition or donation prior to the deadline.
- ○ I tip 25 percent when the service was awful and tell the server why.
- ○ I tithe 10 percent to church, charity, friends, or those who have made me successful.
- ○ I buy the brands I want; I buy the best.

D. Energy and Vitality

Number of circles checked (15 max) _____

- ○ I get a massage or other body work done monthly.
- ○ My blood work shows all normal range results.
- ○ I eat only the foods that nourish me.
- ○ People remark weekly how well I look or how I glow.
- ○ I am never ill.
- ○ I wouldn't even think of tolerating anything, any time, and I am beyond suffering about stuff.
- ○ I consistently underpromise and overdeliver.
- ○ Adrenaline never courses through my veins.
- ○ My need #1 (_____) is fully satisfied.
- ○ My need #2 (_____) is fully satisfied.
- ○ My need #3 (_____) is fully satisfied.
- ○ My Clean Sweep score is 100 out of 100.
- ○ I take four relaxing vacations per year.
- ○ I print out my monthly personal or business financial statement by the 15th of the next month.
- ○ At the end of the business day, I am energized; work and play are the same.

E. Opportunities and Momentum

Number of circles checked (15 max) _____

○ I am at the center of a very strong network.
○ I look forward to each evening.
○ I can call someone for a quick $10,000 loan.
○ My vision is simple and being realized.
○ My three standards are clear and honored.
○ I have what's called the "edge."
○ I have more than enough time to focus solely on my passions.
○ My basic message is crystal clear to all I meet.
○ I discern and tell people who they are.
○ I make huge, strong requests that are accepted.
○ I initiate: I do not hope or wait, ever.
○ I have the ideal life.
○ I am not attached to any result.
○ I can afford to make a million mistakes.
○ People include me in business deals and opportunities.

F. Source and Power

Number of circles checked (15 max) _____

○ My #1 value (_____) is fully honored.
○ My #2 value (_____) is fully honored.
○ My #3 value (_____) is fully honored.
○ I always maintain a strong sense of inner peace.
○ I no longer have to prove myself; I am enough.
○ I am certain I am at choice about my entire life.
○ I honor and respond immediately to my inner voice.
○ I have a strong and personal theme for this year.
○ I am unafraid. I am confident.
○ I act based on desire, not consequence.
○ Nothing hooks me.
○ I self-create and self-manage.
○ I trust a higher power (or myself).
○ I am content with myself; I don't need anyone else to feel healthy or whole.
○ I completely trust my judgment but often ask for others' input.

G. Bonus 10

Number of circles checked (10 max) _____

○ I have more than enough _____.

○ I have more than enough _____.

○ I have more than enough _____.

○ I have more than enough _____.

○ I have more than enough _____.

○ I have more than enough _____.

○ I have more than enough _____.

○ I have more than enough _____.

○ I have more than enough _____.

○ I have more than enough _____.

Intellectual Property Notice

Personal Foundation Program

Personal Foundation is a self-paced personal development program for the individual who wants more—much more—in life and understands the value of investing in oneself by strengthening what we call one's personal foundation.

A personal foundation has 10 parts—each distinct, yet interrelated—forming a solid base on which to develop a most wonderful, satisfying, and fulfilling life. Also, this program requires work on several other programs, notably Clean Sweep, Tru Values, and NeedLess.

The 10 areas that you will be working on are:

- Clearing unresolved matters
- Restoring your integrity
- Getting all of your needs met
- Extending your boundaries
- Raising your personal standards
- Eliminating what you are tolerating
- Coming from positives
- Resolving key family relationships
- Developing a supportive community
- Reorienting around your Tru Values

This is a fairly rigorous program. Take it one piece at a time. Your first score may be less than 10 or 20. Do not worry. You'll get to 70, 80, or 90+ sooner than you may think. Once started, the personal foundation process carries on its own momentum.

Instructions

There are four steps to completing the **Personal Foundation** program.

Step 1: Answer each question.

If the statement is true, fill in the circle. If not, leave it blank until you've done what it takes. Be rigorous; be a hard grader. If the item does not apply or will never be true for you, give yourself credit. (You may do this with up to five items.) Feel free to rewrite or reword up to five of the items in this program to better suit you, your needs, and your life.

Step 2: Summarize each section.

Add up the number of checked circles for each of the 10 sections and write those amounts where indicated. Then add up all 10 sections and write the current total in the progress chart provided.

Step 3: Color in the checklist provided.

If you have five circles checked in the Clearing Unresolved Matters section, color in the bottom five boxes of column A, and so on. Always work from the bottom up. The goal is to have the entire chart filled in. This will indicate how strong your personal foundation is. In the meantime, you have a current picture of how you are doing in each of the 10 areas.

Step 4: Keep playing until all the boxes are filled in.

This process takes between six months and five years, but you can do it! Use your coach to assist you. Check back quarterly for maintenance.

Progress Chart

Date	Points (+/−)	Score

Personal Foundation Program 100-Point Checklist

					Sections					
#	A	B	C	D	E	F	G	H	I	J
10										
9										
8										
7										
6										
5										
4										
3										
2										
1										

Give yourself credit as you get points on the 100-point program. Fill in columns from the bottom up.

A. Clearing Unresolved Matters

Past experiences—what we did, didn't do, should have done, did poorly or wrongly—are always with us in some way. In this section, you get clear of the past, doing what you can and letting go of the rest. You are not your past, yet you may still be living as if you are.

When clearing unresolved matters with the past, a person:
- Feels free of what he or she has done, yet responsible for it all
- Can be with themselves, as they are today, with no compensating
- Is able to set goals and reach them more easily

What happens when one isn't clear:
- One continues to repeat the past in some new way.
- One is reacting to life's unresolved matters instead of flowing with it.

The 10 Steps to Clearing Unresolved Matters

Number of circles checked (10 max) _____

○ Develop strong compassion for yourself: understand that we always do our best, even when we know we aren't.

○ Come to see how staying unresolved with someone or something in your past gives you unhealthy energy.

○ Come to recognize the six signs of being unresolved: regret, remorse, shame, anger, denial, continuing sadness.

○ Make a list of at least 50 things you have left unresolved and start working that list down until it is at zero!

○ Take the Clean Sweep program and work it until your score is above 95.

○ Make a list of the 10 actions you took against others or lies you told; then communicate them fully.

○ In your "clearing" conversations, expect nothing of the other person; it's about you clearing, not their response.

○ Start doing the maximum in work in your tasks, conversations, and actions, so that nothing comes back to bite you for five years.

○ With someone you really trust, share the five things about you that you feel worst about and/or that are your biggest secrets.

○ Make five changes to prevent unresolved matters from occurring.

B. Restore Integrity

To be our best, we must be whole: that is, be responsible for our actions and inactions, respond fully to the lessons being offered to us, honor our bodies and our selves, and respect the realities of the physical universe.

When a person is "in integrity":
- He or she experiences fewer problems.
- Consistent feelings of peace, health, and emotional balance are present.
- He or she reacts to others very little.

What happens when one is "out of integrity":
- Disturbances occur regularly.
- Others are blamed, criticized; one reacts a lot to others.

The 10 Steps to Restoring Integrity Wholeness

Number of circles checked (10 max) _____

○ Make a list of the 10 ways you are currently not in integrity.

○ Get to the source of each and every item; resolve all fully.

○ Dedicate yourself to start living in integrity, as you see it.

○ Let go of at least 10 shoulds, coulds, woulds, oughts, and wills.

○ Involve a coach or other strong, able person to help you.
○ Start getting 50 percent more reserve than you feel you need.
○ Get your score up to 95+ on the Reserves Index program.
○ Stop hanging out with people who are not the best models.
○ Eliminate adrenaline and other unhealthy rushes in your life.
○ Let go of everything that you know is not good for you.

C. Get Your Needs Met

We know we all need air, water, shelter, and food—these are our physical needs. But what about our personal needs? These are things we must have to be ourselves but somehow have not been able to get enough of. Now, it is possible to get enough.

When a person is getting their needs fully met:
- He or she has room and love for other people; there is no competing.
- He or she has a dramatic sense of self-confidence without arrogance.
- Wants naturally decrease: There are no compulsions or musts.

What happens when one's needs are not met:
- Much time is wasted trying to get needs partially met.
- One attracts needy people.

The 10 Steps to Getting Your Needs Met

Number of circles checked (10 max) _____

○ Identify your top four personal needs using the NeedLess program.
○ Ask four special people to each meet one need fully.
○ Train, manage, and coach them to do so until it is done right.
○ Understand that personal needs are fully satisfiable.
○ Set up a SASS (see NeedLess) for each of your four needs.
○ Understand that people who love you will meet your needs.
○ See the difference between neediness and needs satisfaction.
○ When it is true, assert that your personal needs are met.
○ Extend a boundary that will help you satisfy two needs.
○ Ask three friends to tell you what they see your needs to be.

D. Extend Boundaries

Boundaries are imaginary lines we establish around ourselves to protect our souls, hearts, and minds from the unhealthy or damaging behavior of others. It is recommended that you extend your boundaries at least two or three times beyond where they are currently.

When a person has healthy boundaries:

- Fear diminishes significantly; trust is rarely an issue.
- Willing, healthy family members and true friends respect the person.
- The person starts growing more emotionally and developmentally.

What happens when one's boundaries are weak:

- The person attracts needy, disrespectful people into his or her life.
- The person wastes energy keeping life going.

The 10 Steps to Having Extensive Boundaries

Number of circles checked (10 max) _____

- ○ Understand that you need to dramatically extend your boundaries.
- ○ Be willing to educate others how to respect your new boundaries.
- ○ Be relentless, yet not punitive, as you extend boundaries.
- ○ Make a list of the 10 things that people may no longer do around you, do to you, or say to you.
- ○ Sit down with each person involved and share with them your process; get an agreement to honor you.
- ○ Require that every single person in your life is always unconditionally constructive in every single comment to you: no more digs, make-funs, deprecating remarks, criticisms—no matter who or what or the situation!
- ○ Have and use a four-step plan of action whenever someone violates your boundaries: Inform them what they are doing, implore that they stop immediately, require that they stop, walk away without any snappy or get-even comments.
- ○ Make a list of 10 ways you are violating others' boundaries.
- ○ Stop violating the boundaries on that list.
- ○ Reward and congratulate those who are respecting boundaries.

E. Raise Standards

Personal standards refer to the behavior and actions you are willing to hold yourself to. You'll find as you work on the first four areas of the personal foundation program that you'll much more easily expect (and enjoy) more of yourself and of your behavior.

When people have and honor high standards:

- They feel very, very good about themselves, and others, too.
- They become irresistibly attractive to high-quality people.
- They don't get near people or situations that cause problems.

What happens when one's standards are too low:

- One continues to operate "below the line" emotionally.
- Self-esteem drops; self-worth is questioned.

The 10 Steps to Raising Personal Standards

Number of circles checked (10 max) _____

- ○ Make a list of 10 people you admire. Identify their admirable qualities, natural behavior, and how they handle tough situations and people. What standards could you raise that would make you more like them, yet still be you, today?
- ○ Start being unconditionally constructive every single time you open your mouth, yet still say all you need to say.
- ○ Stop spreading gossip, good or bad, about anyone.
- ○ Let go of the standards you believe you should have; make a list of the 10 standards you most want and are ready for today.
- ○ Understand that standards are a choice, not a requirement.
- ○ Fully respond to everything that occurs in your space; assume you had something to do with it, but don't take the blame. Just handle it and raise your standards so it doesn't happen again.
- ○ Always put people and relationships ahead of results.
- ○ Always put your integrity first, needs second, and wants third.
- ○ Understand that others are right, and so are you.
- ○ Always maintain a reserve of time, money, love, and wellness.

F. Stop Tolerating

Humans tolerate a lot. Often, we're taught not to complain, to accept that life is difficult, not to rock the boat, to go along with others, to be grateful for what we have, to be understanding. Not bad advice, but we can still stop tolerating what is bugging us!

When people have stopped tolerating:

- They are happier, more fun to be around.
- They have extra energy to express our values versus our egos.
- They have the edge: we step over nothing.

What happens when they tolerate?

- They and our work become mediocre; we are tired.
- Natural creativity is squashed.

The 10 Steps to a Toleration-Free Life

Number of circles checked (10 max) _____

- ○ Understand that putting up with things is good for no one.
- ○ Make a list of 10 things you are tolerating at home.
- ○ Make the requests or take the actions to eliminate these items.
- ○ Make a list of 10 things you are tolerating at work.
- ○ Take the actions to eliminate these items.
- ○ Understand that you're getting juiced (negatively energized) by tolerating things.

○ Be focused on being toleration free.
○ Stop complaining; instead, make a strong request.
○ Invest $1,000 to handle the tasks or chores that pain you.
○ Do steps 1–9 again after you've done them once!

G. Come from Positives

There is a wonderful feeling that comes from making the shift from focusing on the problems in life to realizing that life is pretty good. This shift may take time, development, and a high score on the Personal Foundation program, but you'll get there! We promise!

When people come from a positive place in life:
- They still live in reality but choose to live a better way.
- They create more positive things happening to us.

What happens until one makes this shift:
- Nothing is good enough, especially oneself.
- Problems are attracted, like bees to honey.

The 10 Shifts to Make to Come from This Place

Number of circles checked (10 max) _____

○ From feeling that one doesn't have enough to being enormously grateful, always
○ From having problems to being a problem-free zone
○ From just getting by to having a healthy reserve of time, love, money, and space
○ From fighting, resisting, and denying the circumstances, problems, and disturbances in life to realizing that you had a lot to do with whatever is happening
○ From doubting yourself to trusting your inklings and intuition
○ From being complacent to making the choice to be fully alive
○ From being passive and waiting to always initiating, being at cause, and creating your life
○ From putting others first to becoming healthfully selfish
○ From talking or being "about" life to being actively "for" life
○ From thinking you're alone to developing a relationship with God, self, spirit, soul (or whatever term you wish)

H. Strengthen Family

Family, whether biological or chosen, is an important part of our personal foundation. Why? Because we need to know we belong, that we are loved, that we can afford to take risks in life because we know there are key people behind and with us.

When a person has a strong family:
- More needs are met, automatically.
- Values are expressed more often.

What happens if one doesn't have a strong family:
- One doubts oneself more often.

The 10 Steps to Strengthening Your Family

Number of circles checked (10 max) _____

- ○ I understand that families are people, not perfect, probably learning how to be better, not there to give me everything I deserve or need; they need love and support from me.
- ○ I've done everything possible to restore any family relationships that hurt me. It is okay with me not to spend time with family members who pain me.
- ○ I have owned up to my role in problems between me and other family members.
- ○ I operate from choice versus obligation or duty when doing things for my family.
- ○ I have nothing negative or unresolved with any of my children.
- ○ I have nothing negative or unresolved with my spouse or mate.
- ○ I have nothing negative or unresolved with an ex.
- ○ I have nothing negative or unresolved with a parent.
- ○ I have nothing negative or unresolved with a relative.
- ○ I have nothing negative or unresolved with a sibling.

I. Strong Community

Nothing worth doing is worth doing alone. Given that, it helps to have a strong personal and professional community: people you can share your love, life, dreams, and concerns with at a level of intimacy once reserved for family.

When people have a strong community:
- They are well-rounded and well-connected; we have a reserve in case of trouble.
- It expands our personal and professional horizons.
- We move in new, more rewarding directions.

What happens if one doesn't have a community:
- One relies excessively on family members to meet needs.
- One misses out on opportunities for personal or professional growth

The 10 Steps to Developing a Community

Number of circles checked (10 max) _____

○ I have a best friend.
○ I have a soul mate.
○ I have at least 10 social friends who I enjoy.
○ I have a successful professional network of at least 25 folks.
○ I contribute daily (in some way) to people in my community.
○ I am loved by people in my community.
○ My friends are happy and healthy; they don't "need" me.
○ I feel good enough about myself to be part of a community.
○ I actively seek out people whose company I enjoy.
○ I can and do say no to people who want to be a part of my community but with whom I do not feel comfortable.

J. Reorient on Values

As you strengthen your personal foundation, you'll find yourself having a lot more time, energy, and space in your life. What should you do with this? Start fully expressing yourself by setting goals based on your Tru Values.

When people orient around their values:
- Goal setting is easier and goals are reached more quickly.
- Our life purpose or vision comes to us clearly.
- Fewer distractions occur; life is simple but rich.

What happens until one does this:
- They are frustrated in the area of goals and lack a strong reference point in life.
- Their goals, wants, and ideas keep changing.

The 10 Steps to Fully Expressing Your Values

Number of circles checked (10 max) _____

○ Read through and complete the Tru Values program worksheet.
○ Understand that you are your Tru Values and that expressing these values is what will make you feel fulfilled in life.
○ Understand that goals are more fun when linked to your values.
○ Identify 10 key Tru Values: set one goal to match each value.
○ Let go of goals that can't be linked to one of the 10 Tru Values (unless they strengthen your personal foundation).
○ Begin working on each of these 10 goals immediately.
○ Reach each of these 10 goals.
○ Identify your number one value: your key value.

○ Raise a personal standard through the roof in order to help you more fully orient around your key value.

○ Discover your life purpose as expressed by your number one value.

Intellectual Property Notice

This material and these concepts are the intellectual property of Coach U, Inc. You may not repackage or resell this program without express written authorization and royalty payment. The exception is that you may deliver this program to single individuals without authorization or fee. If you lead a workshop or develop or deliver a program to a group or company based on or including this material or these concepts, authorization and fees are required. You may make as many copies of this program as you wish, as long as you make no changes or deletions of any kind.

Resources

Attention Readers:

Thank you for participating in the collective wisdom of Coach U. Together, we all continue to learn. Additional resources and forms can be found in the *Coach U's Essential Coaching Tools: Your Complete Practice Resource* book by Coach U, Inc.

Attention CoachInc.com Students and Graduates:

CoachinInc.com students and graduates may find additional and/or more recent resources associated with this module in the resource area of the student-only website. If you are a student or graduate of one of CoachInc.com's ICF-accredited coach training programs, you can access these by searching under the name of the course. When the course description page appears you may find a link to the list of additional resources. Each item is a live link to its actual location on the website. Click on the item to access the information.

Do remember to take the associated online self-test for this module once you have completed the course in-person or by TeleClass. The tests are required for coach certification with the International Coach Federation. Throughout the course or anytime you find valuable resources for a particular course, please feel free to add to the value of our curriculum by forwarding the resource to revampteam@coachu.com.

Notes

Notes

Coach U, Inc. Intellectual Property Rights

The following are the intended guidelines as to what you may and may not do with the Coach U, Inc. created materials, concepts, tools, processes, and programs. We encourage you to use many of the Coach U, Inc. programs and materials in ways that benefit you, your coachees, and your business. We are committed to your satisfaction and support as someone who is interested in Coach training and the profession of Coaching, so please read these guidelines with that in mind. If you have further questions or need additional support, please email licensing@coachu.com with your question or request.

THE BASIC INTELLECTUAL PROPERTY RIGHTS:

As an original purchaser of this material you are granted a license to use, not ownership of, specific materials and programs that are a part of Intellectual Property of Coach U, Inc. A license grants permission to use the selected programs and materials in approved ways.

Individual Use:
Coaches may use/duplicate/share/teach all of the "Coachee Coaching Programs" to anyone, group or individual, in a TeleClass, onsite, live workshop or live presentation, with no royalty due to Coach U, Inc. or permission required. This includes programs such as the Clean Sweep, 25 Secrets, Personal and Professional Foundation, and Irresistible Attraction, etc. When using the material, the integrity of the material needs to remain intact and the creation/copyright/contact information for Coach U, Inc MUST be included in use of the material (sample: copyright, 2005 Coach U, Inc.com, all rights reserved. www.coachu.com).

Use for the Training of Coaches:
If it is your intention to use these materials as curriculum for the training of coaches we ask that you request permission from Coach U, Inc. as original authors of this intellectual property. Our intention in making this request is not to restrict the use of the materials in any way but to support you in creating training programs that maintain the integrity of our intellectual property. Such requests can be made by sending an email to licensing@coachu.com.

Interested in Learning More?

We primarily provide coach training to individuals wishing to become certified coaches. We also offer other coach training, personal development, and professional development programs to individuals and organizations in person and through distance learning using the internet and TeleClasses.

Interested in Bringing Coaching to Your Organization?

If you would like to learn more about creating a coaching culture within your organization or having us speak at one of your organization's events, we would be happy to discuss this with you. We are experienced in providing customized coach training programs, individual and group coaching services, and can also consult with you to develop other customized programs.

Interested in Hiring a Coach?

Our International Coach directory contains listings of hundreds of Coach U and Corporate Coach U trained coaches located throughout the world. For information on how to hire a coach or to view profiles of coaches complete with contact information, please visit www.findacoach.com.

Don't forget to request your complimentary copy of our book *Becoming A Coach.*

Contact Us Today

1-800-48COACH
admissions@coachinc.com
www.coachinc.com
www.ccui.com / www.coachu.com

CoachInc.com
P.O. Box 881595
Steamboat Springs, CO 80488-1595

We Want Your Feedback!

We appreciate the opportunity to act upon your feedback. Whether you would like to share a positive review, provide constructive criticism, offer suggestions, or would simply like to share how this publication has made an impact on you or your organization, we want to hear from you. Thank you in advance!

Jennifer Corbin
President of Coach U and Corporate Coach U
jennifer@coachinc.com
1-800-329-5655